GW01466488

The Rent-to-Rent Blueprint II

Real Life Experiences

Napa Bafikele

Napa Bafikele

First published in 2020 by Napa Bafikele

ISBN: 979-8638438-82-1

Disclaimer

The author does not accept any liability in the event of any type of loss or damage which may be incurred, directly or indirectly, as a consequence from the application of any content contained in this book.

Within you is the spring of life. In your light, we see light.

Psalms 36:9 (CEB)

Dedication

I would especially like to dedicate this book to my grandfather Antoine Nsakala Bay Nkondani. Your ethics and morals are truly inspirational. Thank you for the care and love you freely gave me during my formative years. You are the spirit behind the man I am today.

I would also like to dedicate this book to my grandparents Ivon Bafikele, Adeline Mukaripay and Veronique Manvibidila. Although we never met, may your souls rest in peace, your legacy laid the spiritual foundation for my growth and development.

Acknowledgements

I would like to thank my mentees Steven Fontaine, Dylan Fontaine, Kenan Buckley, Richard Greeves, Carol Mbaya, Kyle Hart, Duquarne Edwards, Chun-Eu Man and Jake Aldric for sharing their stories and experiences. I would also like to thank Mitesh Parmar for his valued contribution.

My gratitude to my dad Macaire Bafikele, mum Wivine Bay Nsakala, my brother Pathy Bafikele, my sisters Pamela Bayilema, Beryl Bafikele and for your love, support and encouragement. My daughter Eden-Destiny Bafikele for bringing joy into my life and reinforcing my purpose on this planet. Special thank you to my partner Milvia Serra.

I would like to thank my editor Vinette Hoffman-Jackson for her advice and assistance. I would also like to thank Marco Mukendi, Gomer Lukisa and many others that supported me.

Finally, my sincerest gratitude to everyone, friends and acquaintances, who supported me by purchasing a copy of this book or offered other support on my journey, whether directly or indirectly. I truly appreciate your input. You the reader I would also like to thank you.

FOREWORD

The Rent-To-Rent Blueprint Book 2 (Real life experiences) provides people with the practical tools they need to develop or start their own property business through the lessons learnt from the experiences of the people that have benefitted from Napa's mentorship in the property industry.

It also reinforces the importance of having a mentor who is fully equipped with the right information that you need to help you get started on your own rent-to-rent journey.

In this book, Napa also impresses upon us the central idea that working nine to five for financial freedom is a fallacy and is almost impossible to achieve. He, however, provides the option of harnessing the transferrable skills you may learn and applying them to property investment to increase your probability of success.

He explores the importance of having a growth mindset as the ultimate key to sustained success. Yes, hard work, effort, and persistence are all important, but not as important as having that underlying belief that you are in control of your own life and destiny.

If you are one of those people who wants to be in control of your own life and destiny then this book is written for you. You have not picked up this book by accident. You have not wandered here aimlessly. With this tool in your hand, this could be the step that you have been missing to start your own rent-to-rent business.

Claver Lukoki

The author of "The purpose of Existence" book and the founder of B.M.A Foundation.

The Rent-to-Rent Blueprint II

Real Life Experiences

Table of Contents

Introduction

In my previous book, *The Rent-to-Rent Blueprint,* I introduced the concept of starting your rent-to-rent journey and provided easy practical steps that you could use to run a successful rent-to-rent business. I included valuable information that most property gurus fail to mention and the likely pitfalls you could potentially face. If you are a newbie to this property strategy, I would strongly recommend you start by reading *The Rent-to-Rent Blueprint* first, before reading this book.

Working a nine to five job has its pros and cons. Some people enjoy their job however, some people do not enjoy their jobs. Being dissatisfied with your work can lead to several health-related problems and serious mental health issues. Yet, very few people are likely to look at alternatives and try to save themselves. They find a job and settle in their comfort zone under the guise of job security.

Most people will never live the life of their dreams or live according to their purpose. They believe they need to work hard in order to make money to survive. According to a survey conducted by CareerBuilder, almost one third of British workers live from paycheck to paycheck. I personally believe that figure to be higher. In fact, some people cannot make it from paycheck to paycheck. They rely on borrowing from Peter to pay Paul, shifting credit card balances and sinking deeper into debt each passing month.

Rent-to-Rent is a property strategy that allows you to control someone else's asset and make substantial profit from it. Anyone can start a rent-to-rent business, **but it is not for everyone.** In addition, not everyone is cut to be an entrepreneur or businessmen or women.

I want you to imagine what you would do if you had a steady and substantial cash flow. Would you travel the world? Would you embark on a journey that is more meaningful? Would you become a philanthropist? Whatever you envisioned, if you do rent-to-rent correctly, you can achieve all those dreams.

The main aim of this book is to highlight the practical element of rent-to-rent through the experiences of people I have trained and mentored. The book is also written to give you a feel and an insight of what it could be like if you were properly trained, mentored and equipped with the right tools to embark on your own rent-to-rent journey. I want you to get a deeper understanding of the rent-to-rent strategy as seen through the eyes of my mentees while reading their stories, sharing their experiences and celebrating their success and lessons learned.

You will also learn about how to tap into your inner self and become unstoppable, creating the right mindset for your rent-to-rent journey. You will learn various techniques employed by my mentees, that you can incorporate into your own rent-to-rent business to enhance its performance and set you apart from your competition.

Anyone who wants to take control of their own destiny, their finances, to live life at their own terms, be their own boss, take calculated risks and finally become the leader they dreamt about, then this book is for you. This book will help you by sharpening your mindset, attitude and expectations towards the rent-to-rent strategy. In the words of Les Brown 'It is possible!' and this book will show you how.

Chapter I

Mamba Attitude

"A lot of people say they want to be great, but they're not willing to make the sacrifices necessary to achieve greatness."
— ***Kobe Bryant***

In January 2020, I decided to celebrate my birthday in Dubai and had an amazing time. My partner and I returned to the UK on the 26th January and we were met by one of my dearest friends. We got busy chatting and joking around on the drive home. I was so caught up in the conversation that I did not pay any attention to where we were heading. The car suddenly stopped at a venue in Wood Green, North London. Before I could ask any questions, my partner and friend alighted from the vehicle. Their coordinated actions told me something was up, so I played along. We walked into the restaurant where I saw a group of my closest friends.

Unknowing to me, my partner had arranged a surprise birthday meal. I felt touched, humbled and loved. The emotions were intense. I was grateful that people had taken time from their busy schedules to celebrate my birthday.

During the meal, one of my property friends said, 'You won't believe what I'm about to say!' I looked at him quizzically, smiled and asked him to go ahead. He said, 'Kobe Bryant is dead'. This guy has always been a playful character, so I did not believe him. He then showed me a piece of evidence and I googled it and found it was true.

I was gobsmacked. I had random thoughts rushing through my head. I thought to myself, I was also on a flight that day and it could have been me. Was I ready to go? Would I be remembered? Would I be missed? It may seem surreal, but that news shook me to the core and altered my outlook on life.

I knew Kobe Bryant was an amazing basketball player, but I did not follow basketball off the courts. I did not know much about the man and the life he led. This opened an opportunity for me to do more research about the man behind the name. The more I read, the more intrigued I became. The information I discovered opened my mind to a different level of thinking.

If you read a thousand books or speak to a thousand people on the topic of success, you will find one word, one concept and one value that keeps repeating itself. **That is attitude!**

Attitude is defined as a settled way of thinking or feeling about something. This is a very important character trait in the determination of your level of success.

As a property mentor and a coach, most times I can predict who will be successful and who will not be, based on their initial attitude. Some mentees I train always seem to find an excuse or reason why they are not achieving the task I have set them. They will focus on the problem instead of trying to find possible solutions. This poor attitude holds them back and slows their overall progress.

Kobe Bryant crafted and perfected his unique attitude for success and branded it *'mamba mentality'*. His mamba mentality was birthed when the athlete was at his lowest point in life, both professionally and personally. Kobe decided to create an alter – ego that allowed him to become unstoppable. I was fascinated and wanted to find out what was so special about the black mamba that caught his attention.

The black mamba is Africa's longest, fastest and most venomous snake. It is one of the fastest snakes in the world reaching speeds of up to twelve and a half miles per hour. The black mamba can strike with ninety nine percent accuracy at maximum speed.

It is not hard to see why Kobe chose this animal to represent his new attitude to life. Adapting the unique traits of the black mamba as a foundation to build your attitude to life, means you can potentially achieve any goal you set.

Let us break down the key characteristics of a black mamba and how you can use these to your advantage.

Speed:

As one of the fastest snakes in the world, it can catch almost any prey.

As a rent-to-rent entrepreneur or business operator, speed is crucial, almost a vital necessity.

At the beginning of my property journey, the first letting agent I dealt with told me 'You snooze, you lose!' and I have never forgotten this phrase or the implications for my business. I had arranged to view a property in a carefully researched and selected area. I was eager and arrived five minutes earlier than the agreed time. The agent was already in the middle of showing someone else around the same property, so I sat and waited in my car. As soon as I saw the person leaving, I immediately got out of my car and headed towards the property. As I got closer to the door, the agent walked out and closed the door behind him. I informed him that my viewing was at six o' clock and I was on time. He then explained to me that the person that had viewed the property before me, made an offer and paid everything right there and then. The property was now off the market. I was livid. I felt like I had wasted my time and effort. I realised then, that speed was a necessity to secure property deals.

If you intend to operate in London or any major metropolitan area, speed is a must, otherwise you will keep missing deals. The property investment business can be described as a savage industry. It generally operates on a first come first serve basis. Unless you have previously established a great relationship with the agent or landlord, you can miss a deal in a fraction of a second if someone makes an offer before you and it is accepted.

If you are limited in terms of the time you have to invest in this business, then speed becomes even more of an essential skill to achieve more in the short period of time you have available.

I spent a couple of hours with one of my mentees as he was struggling to arrange viewings with agents. Mindful that he works full time, I knew the importance of ensuring that every free minute he could spare was used efficiently. He had to work quickly to identify potential investment properties then arrange viewings. I asked him to take me through the process of finding a property and contacting agents. I observed that it took him approximately fifteen minutes to identify a property on Rightmove, qualify it, then contact the agent. His conversations with agents ranged from eight to ten minutes per call. Based on my calculations, in the space of an hour he only contacted two to three agents. This is a poor work rate when you are trying to arrange viewings and time is against you. In the competitive world of rent-to-rent you would have limited chances against a full-time entrepreneur.

To improve your speed; first, create a spreadsheet of all property types in your area. The majority of property types will have a similar asking price in the same area. Secondly, find out what are the estimated room rates for double, single, and premium rooms for couples or those with en suites. Thirdly, become familiar with the transportation system and the location of key amenities in that area.

I usually budget £100 per room for bills until I do my in-depth due diligence and get actual quotes. Once I have collated all this information and put it into my spreadsheet it saves me time. The spreadsheet gives me the speed to quickly determine whether a property is a great deal or not. It provides me with the basic information to negotiate. I can also quickly assess whether I will need an additional room to make a certain property type work and factor this into any discussion.

For example, I will analyse my profit margin with a three-bedroom property and if there is no margin, I will look at three-bedroom properties with additional living space to see if I could convert a reception room and create a workable margin.

Always work to identify potential properties a day before. The following day should be spent contacting agents to arrange viewings. This will save you a lot of time on the day instead of sitting around and browsing trying to see if the property is a fit for your business strategy.

When you are contacting agents or landlords, arrange to view the property immediately. This may not always be possible for people working in fulltime employment but where there is a will there is a way. Everyone still has only twenty-four hours each day. If possible, negotiate your hours with your boss by working through your lunch times and taking the hour at the end of the day or starting early and finishing early. You could potentially call at the end of the workday on Friday and arrange to have the first viewings on Saturday morning. As offices usually close at five o' clock, there is no risk of someone jumping ahead of you. These are techniques you can use to better position yourself for success.

I have focussed on the importance of speed but there is another element that works in synchronicity, and that is accuracy. Moving quickly, should not be at the expense of accuracy. You could view a thousand properties first but close very few deals. The preparation you do behind the scenes, including the spreadsheet, will help you to improve your accuracy. Aim only for your target properties and not every available option. This will help you to become more focussed and lead to more successes. The successes you achieve will also be a psychological boost and drive you towards even greater success in this business. Nothing compares to that feeling when you close a deal, except maybe closing two deals.

Agility:

I studied for a Sport and Exercise Science degree and part of the assessment process involved how to analyse an athlete's agility. Agility is defined as your ability to change direction quickly while maintaining total control of your body or movement. The black mamba is a masterclass in agility, making it extremely dangerous to its prey.

How can we relate this to property investment? Agility extends beyond the control of your body movement;

it extends to your flexibility and communication skills in a fast pace market.

There are no books or mentors that can explore every potential obstacle you might face in business. It is an impossible task. The recent outbreak of Covid-19 is the perfect example. No one could have predicted the global impact and the effects on your business. This is one of the main reasons that I have included this chapter in a book on rent-to-rent. Mindset, attitude and resilience are key components to cope with your success and navigate unexpected occurrences.

You must be flexible and willing to adapt to changing circumstances.

I once heard a story about a conversation between a mighty oak tree and the lowly bamboo plant. The oak tree boasted to the little bamboo 'I am so big and strong nothing can move me. My dear bamboo I am afraid you will not last long because you are not as tall and rooted as deeply as I am'. The bamboo said nothing. Later that night there was a huge storm with hurricane winds that blew hard. The oak tree would not be moved and stood rooted, not bending in the wind. The bamboo on the other hand swayed to and fro, bending with the direction of each wind change. When the night finally ended and dawn appeared, a sad sight greeted the bamboo. The mighty oak had fallen onto its side leaving the bamboo upright and standing tall. The moral of the story, it is okay to bend sometimes to prevent yourself from breaking. Be flexible in business.

As a property entrepreneur I know what I want before I start my negotiations, but I am always flexible to accommodate a new suggestion or offer as long as it does not impact my profit margins significantly.

We communicate both verbally and non-verbally everyday both in our personal and professional life. Your ability to communicate skilfully and in most cases in impromptu settings can separate you from the competition.

As a property investor, there will be occasions where you are left feeling frustrated or even angry, but you must learn to control your temper and manage your emotions. The agent or landlord that upset you today could be the ones you work with in the future.

It is impossible for you to know everything about everything. At some point along your journey a question, a casual comment or a directive will leave you at a loss for words. It could be a question about an aspect of your business strategy, a comment about how you have dealt with a crisis or an instruction to do something and you do not have sufficient knowledge to execute. Your agile response may save the deal. This is a skill I believe all politicians learn very quickly. To remain unperturbed in tricky conversations with investors, landlords or tenants you must be attentive, especially when you encounter obstacles or unforeseen problems. Most issues that arise in rent-to-rent tend to reoccur. If you learn from each experience you become more adept at solving these issues at a faster pace next time they occur. This will give you a confidence boost and convey to others that you are in control of the situation.

One of my new mentees went out for his first viewing with an agent. The agent asked him what his company did without any warning. As he was new and inexperienced, he suddenly became very anxious as he did not know how to answer this simple question, so he froze.

This type of reaction immediately tells the agent that you are inexperienced, and you do not know how your business operates. This could immediately set off warning flags in the minds of the agent. They may no longer wish to work with you, and you could forfeit the deal. In business, confidence and strong communication skills will trump indecisions and hesitation every time. Any lingering doubt in the mind of an investor or business partner that you might lose their money is an immediate turn off.

However, if the mentee is able to change the direction of the conversation quickly whilst maintaining control, then he could rescue himself and save the deal. The first thing to remember is the importance of preparation, this will ensure you are ready for most questions. A mentor is invaluable in this area. They have done it before so their experience will help you avoid the pitfalls you may encounter. If you do find yourself in this situation, I recommend you switch the conversation by asking about something specific, relating to the property and buy some thinking time to collect your thoughts. You could also use humour to diffuse the tension by asking 'Which one of my businesses?' followed by a chuckle. You will both smile and that will thaw any frigidity and release endorphins that make you both relax. Learn from this experience however and make sure you have the correct answer next time you are asked this question.

You should be able to explain your business in one sentence. The more you talk, the more likely you are to make mistakes or lie. Never lie to get you through the moment. Business lies tend to come back and bite you later.

Be honest and sincere with your responses. One trait that everyone recognises in me is my authenticity. I never pretend to be someone I am not. I am always Napa everyday of every week. I live my brand.

Arboreal vs Terrestrial:

Black mambas are both arboreal and terrestrial in nature, meaning they can live in trees and on the ground. This trait is unique, as few animals can live comfortably in different habitats. This characteristic makes the mamba highly adaptable and extend the boundaries of their hunting zone. It takes a different type of skill to hunt in trees than to hunt on the ground, yet the mamba has mastered both.

Quite frequently I teach my mentees about gold mine areas. These are areas where they can comfortably make a profit from their rent-to-rent business and has long term sustainability. They are classed as gold mine areas because they may have a number of upcoming businesses, government investments or an influx of young professionals gravitating towards that area which makes it a prime area for investment. Gold mine areas are not unique and do not always follow the same criteria, so mentees have to be adaptable and mentally prepared to work hard in different areas.

In a cosmopolitan area, your property may need to be up to a certain specification to attract the type of tenants you want but you may need less marketing as the area is buzzing and people are always looking for properties. On the other hand, a quieter place may need furnishings to be upper echelon, but you need to be relentless in your marketing to get the rooms filled.

As an entrepreneur you must be able to adapt to different scenarios. You must also have foresight to look at potential trends and keep ahead of the curve. If you wait too long the competition increases and you may lose out on major deals. Like the black mamba, take to the trees so you are high above your competitors and you are able to see the bigger picture. This skillset is definitely needed in the post Covid-19 business climate. If you remain at the ground level during this time, you may struggle to see a way out of the dilemma. Fear feeds fear and if everyone around you is panicking then you are more likely to panic or get anxious. Take to the trees and look for opportunities in the middle of the crises. Try to gauge where the market is heading or learn about a new property strategy. Look beyond your current situation and be ready when opportunity knocks.

I joint ventured with one of my mentees whose story is shared in chapter five. His deal required a significant capital investment and most investors were reluctant to engage. The investors failed to scrutinise the deal adequately because he was new to the property arena. Based on the deal structure, capital repayment would not have been affected. My mentee had negotiated a two-month free rental period which translated into solely income, excluding bills for those two months. I invested in his business and within seven months all my cash injection was repaid, now I am receiving passive income from the cashflow generated from the property deal.

Skin Shedding:

Ecdysis is a process that means skin shedding. Snakes shed their old skins to allow further growth and rid itself of parasites. Typically, most species take one to two weeks to shed their skins except the black mamba that can shed theirs in a matter of minutes.

From a biological perspective we all shed the outer layer of our skins although it is much more dramatic in reptiles. On a metaphorical level it is a key feature of business growth and development. We need to shed our old selves, our old mindset and the parasites that become

20

attached to us when we embark on a new business journey. We must shed to become a better version of ourselves.

Property is a business. This is the most undervalued statement that the majority of new property investors fail to comprehend early in their journey. If you conduct your business like a lifestyle, failure is inevitable. A concrete plan must be established before any action commences. Understanding how business operates is crucial for your rent-to-rent or any other property business. If you currently lack the knowledge of the business you must shed that person, learn and become one that fully understand all aspects of this business. Growth in knowledge changes your perspectives and improve your outlook on life.

The mamba also recognises that parasites sometimes attach themselves and the only way to grow is to shed them. I do not have to do any research, contact a psychic or ask any question, but I know that at some point we have all attracted parasites that fed off us financially, emotionally and psychologically, draining our energy and resources and giving nothing back. In creating a business and a new version of yourself you have to be firm and let the parasites go. Leave relationships that no longer serve you, move away from people who take and do not give and surround yourself with people on the same mission as yourself.

At the early stage of my journey, I did not take this industry as a business because the trainers and mentors seldomly included this in their presentations. I just wanted to create a cashflow to fund my lifestyle. However, further down my property journey, my business suffered as I did not have the correct skills and knowledge to manage a growing property business. Growth always brings discomfort. This is something you need to be aware of and adapt quickly. As we often hear, there is no growth in the comfort zone. In every aspect of life, growth is painful, but the rewards far exceed the discomfort.

As you are in the process of skin shedding there are several areas, I want to you to pay close attention to. This will help you on your journey.

Pressure and emotions:

Rent-to-rent is demanding and challenging. If it was not, everyone would be doing it. Since it does not require a lot of capital to get started, it is quite attractive to most people. Over the last five years I have seen a significant increase in the number of people doing rent-to-rent. Should this turn you off? Absolutely not! In reality, there are not many people doing it correctly. If you position your business correctly you could definitely outperform the competition.

Successfully handling pressure and emotion will also determine your progress in this business. It is a pressurised environment with many commitments that often requires your time, attention and effort simultaneously. It sometimes feels as if you are juggling five balls and you cannot allow any to fall. For example, whether the property is cash flowing positively or not, you are still obligated to pay the landlord the full rent as agreed on the contract and you are still obligated to pay all the bills. When you have empty rooms, it costs you money and adds an enormous amount of pressure. I am also mindful that unresolved or ongoing issues in your personal life can also impact your business and add another layer of pressure.

Pressure can fuel a lot of negative emotions like stress and fear. If these are not dealt with correctly you could end up suffering serious mental health issues. However, they are not 'bad' emotions. Fear and stress can be positively harnessed and converted to motivation and drive. Imagine yourself jogging just for pleasure then suddenly a lion appears. You will find strength and speed you did not know you had in order to survive. It is very similar in business. You find more energy and focus when you have empty rooms and those bills need to be paid at the end of the month. Your adrenal glands will be stimulated to produce excess adrenaline. At this point you must choose whether to fight or flight.

If the pressure causes your emotions to get out of our control, rational and logical decisions can be affected.

I had a mentee who was very eager to tenant his rent-to-rent property in order to make sure he had enough income to fulfil his monetary obligations. When it did not happen as quickly as he wanted, out of desperation, he ignored the basic guidelines I provided on how to vet a tenant and rented to the first person that expressed interest. The prospective tenant was a man in his fifties and unemployed. He sold my mentee a sad story. He was from a wealthy background and had been left with a huge inheritance that used to fund his retirement. I warned my mentee that I could see lots of red flags but his determination to fill the property quickly prevented him from seeing things from my perspective.

As soon as this tenant moved in, his dream turned into a nightmare. This caused chaos in the property. He encouraged the other tenants to behave obnoxiously towards my mentee. It was a large HMO and the other tenants were in their mid and late twenties. This created a generational gap and some tenants became increasingly uncomfortable and requested to vacate the property urgently. The pressure intensified and as my mentee needed to retain the majority of tenants and keep them happy to minimise his losses, he had to evict the problem tenant prematurely.

As you are growing and shedding old skin, embrace the pressure as it helps you to develop tenacity and resilience, preparing you for the new you.

Venom:

One bite from a black mamba will kill you in less than thirty minutes, unless the antivenom is administered immediately. The venom is so lethal, it makes the black mamba one of the most feared and respected snakes worldwide. Interestingly, few people are attacked by black mambas as its reputation precedes it. In rent-to-rent you must command respect from landlords, agents and tenants. Command but not demand. Rent-to-rent is becoming more popular with an increasing level of competition. You must therefore stand out from your competitors to give you that extra edge that makes agents and landlords want to work with you. You must become highly respected in your field by building a solid reputation that enters any room before you're physically present.

In crafting your reputation, the first thing you need to understand is how your business model works. You must be able to explain to any audience what rent-to-rent is and how it can benefit them. Strive to be an expert in the field. Create value and a unique selling point for your clients that no one else offers.

I once heard a quote 'Observe the masses and do the opposite!' This will certainly help you to stand out. From my own personal observations, more people are exiting property training courses and receiving the same information, which is creating an army of clones in the property industry. These particular individuals will get on the phone and contact agents sounding exactly the same, using the same script.

There is nothing unique about your business if you adhere to this method. It also becomes very repetitive to agents because they are hearing the same script every time. Think of your response when you get a cold call from a call centre. The immediate reaction is to switch off. This has resulted in many agents now saying they do not do corporate or company lets before the pitch is completed. In my mentoring programme I have created key bullet points for my mentees to use in order to create their own script.

The second focus point is your language. The next time you take a sales call from any company, pay close attention to how the caller is pitching to you. The trained salesperson will rarely use the word "I" when talking about the company. Many people who are new to the property arena, make some basic errors when they speak to agents. The typical conversation thread would possibly read; "Hi, I am calling regarding a property I saw on Rightmove that I am interested to rent as a corporate let". How many 'I's' did you count? The moment you start saying "I am interested to rent it as corporate let," it makes the agent question the magnitude and credibility of your company. Using a distinguished well written sales approach while contacting agents helps them to put you in a different category and they are more likely to do business with you. 'I' sounds like an individual trying to gain a few pounds; 'we' sounds like a company that is already trading successfully.

Thirdly, let us consider positioning. Most people present themselves to their audience (landlords, agents or tenants) as the director of the company. There is no obvious harm in that unless it is not true. However, when you are starting your rent-to-rent journey or any business venture you are inexperienced. There will be certain obstacles you have not yet met, but as the director of a company your audience will expect you to know everything. I see this quite often, and it has also happened to me.

At the start of my journey I went to view a property that I really liked on Rightmove. The numbers worked very well based on my online due diligence. I passed the phone stage and managed to arrange a viewing. Once I got to the viewing everything was going well until the agent started questioning me about the business. I had no idea how to respond since I had just started. The agent was very experienced, and this showed in the quality of questions he posed. I was an amateur, completely out of my depths and no business was generated from that agent.

Another obstacle I encountered was a very challenging tenant. Since he was aware that I was the director of the company, it gave me less breathing space and thinking time to come up with a mutually acceptable solution to a problem he wanted solved. He expected an answer immediately.

I experienced many different situations that made me re-evaluate how I positioned myself to my audience. Once I learnt, it made life easier. It gave me space and time to formulate my answers with less pressure. My timely response also reduced the likelihood of making mistakes which helped to build my credibility in the property industry.

People talk, so the chances of your audiences talking about you is very high. Your unique approach, how you speak and the way you position yourself as you conduct business will help build a solid reputation that is celebrated and respected by your audience and feared by your competitors.

Visibility:

Before the black mamba attacks it will raise itself up to approximately four feet in the air to be seen. Most mamba attacks show that they bite the upper torso of the body. The mamba becomes more visible to ward off predators.

In the rent-to-rent business visibility is quite helpful. It will make you a first choice for agents and help to secure tenants quickly. One way of attracting the tenants you want rapidly is to ensure that you are on the first page of all advertisement platforms. You may need to invest more but feature this as part of your marketing expense.

We live in a fast pace world with patience a diminishing virtue. People do not spend time searching for the things they want. Online searchers rarely go to the second or third page for results. You are the perfect subject to evidence this. How often do you click to the second page of google while browsing the net? I presume not many times. The same tendencies apply when prospective tenants are searching for rooms.

Presentation of your company brand will help to distinguish you from competition. Information is readily available than ever in the twenty first century. We all own mobile phones so we can get answers in the blink of an eye. Therefore, your company must have an online presence and it must be presented well. Your branding should be easily identifiable and give information to potential clients about the services you provide.

You may be surprised to learn that the black mamba is not actually black in colour. The snake gets its name from the black colouration inside its mouth. That distinctive feature makes the black mamba memorable. As soon as it opens its mouth you know what to expect. This is the same emotions your brand must convey. People involved directly or indirectly should know what you stand for and what they will get from you.

I did also a joint venture with one of my mentees of an African ethnicity. He went to view a property in South London, and it was estimated to have a cashflow of £880 per month. Since his company was new, the landlord decided to do further research on the company.

The landlord came across my mentee's website that was partially finished. While the landlord was surfing my mentee's website, she clicked on the 'About Us' link and there were only pictures of Caucasian individuals.

Immediately, the landlord became very suspicious and contacted my mentee to ask him; 'Why do you have only Caucasians on your *About Us* link?' My mentee explained that the website was still under construction, but the landlord told him he was misrepresenting himself and being dishonest on his online platform. The deal never went through. My mentee ignored the details I provided about creating his personal brand by uploading free images from the internet. This may not be the end of the world, but it is a lesson worth learning.

Individuality:

Unlike other reptiles, black mambas are solitary creatures who prefer to operate as individuals instead of in herds. You may not know but the black mamba is part of a family of mambas, but it stands out because it is unique.

Undoubtedly there are many positives of operating in partnerships or as part of a team but try and discover yourself first. This is very important. People who do not know who they are tend to follow everyone and disappear in the crowd. You want to stand out.

I do not look like a typical property investor. I look like Napa. Even if I am working as part of a team I stand out. I am an individual. I never realised the importance of this until much later in life. As a young man, one person I looked up to told me I had to cut my braids and wear a suit to be taken seriously as a property entrepreneur. I listened and cut my hair, but I never truly felt comfortable with my appearance. It was not me. I felt I was trying to fit a template created by other businessmen of different backgrounds and with different experiences to my own.

As soon as I discovered who I wanted to be, I confidently represented myself authentically because I now know who I am. Take time to find yourself and remain true to it.

In conclusion, make sure you have the right tools in your arsenal that will make you stand out from your competition, it will separate you from your competitors and make agents and landlords gravitate towards you. Your reputation and fairness will precede you and tenants will want to stay in your properties. Anyone not on their A-game will be left behind.

A bite from you should paralyse or terminate your opponents. Don't be fooled into believing everyone knows their business models and how to work effectively. Some people are just limping along or relying on third parties to carry their businesses. Their intentions, ethics and morals could be misplaced so their tenants do not get a fair deal. People operating at these standards help to paint a bad picture of the rent-to-rent strategy and it creates more resistance from agents and landlords who may want to work with us.

Develop a black mamba attitude and be a person of integrity!

Chapter II

Let your own light shine!

*"As we work to create light for others, we naturally light our own way." – **Mary Anne Radmache***

I remember watching the movie Coach Carter. Towards the last scenes of the movie, one of the characters gave a speech and the words have remained with me since. If you have not seen this movie, it is well worth watching. The protagonist Coach Carter locks the sports hall to stop students from training as they were underperforming in all their classes. This was done at a point when the team was winning all their matches and Coach Carter's decision resulted in the team forfeiting some of their games. He decided to hold this hard line until the team got their grades up. This action caused a lot of parents, fans and teachers to get upset. The faculty decided to bring all the stakeholders together for a vote on whether the gym should remain closed as Coach Carter wished or opened. The majority of the votes were to reopen the gym.

Upon hearing the decision, Coach Carter resigned from his position as the team basketball coach. As he was heading towards the gym to collect his belongings, he saw the chains he had used to lock the gym had been cut and left on the floor. When he stepped into the gym, he saw his players sitting down in a classroom format. One of the players said "Sir, they can cut the chain off the door, but they can't make us play". They were a few more comments, however, the one that stood out for me was the short speech Timo Cruz gave. He said:

"Our deepest fear is not that we are inadequate.

Our deepest fear is that we are powerful beyond measure.

It is our light, not our darkness, that most frightens us.

You're playing small does not serve the world.

There is nothing enlightened about shrinking so that other people won't feel insecure around you.

We are all meant to shine as children do.

It's not just in some of us; it is in everyone.

And as we let our own lights shine, we unconsciously give another person permission to do the same.

As we are liberated from our own fear, our presence automatically liberates others."

This quote has impacted my life in a major way, to the extent that I had it tattooed on my left pectoral.

The line that stood out the most is "As we let our own light shine, we unconsciously give other people permission to do the same". This concept permeated throughout my first book. Once you identify your WHY, your outlook on life changes and that change somehow directly or indirectly impact others around you. You become more focussed and people around you see that and feel inspired to do the same.

Your WHY gives you a purpose in life. Finding your why is a process of self-discovery which helps you identify your strengths and weakness so that you can work on yourself and become a better version each day. You start to grow into your purpose.

A good friend of mine Claver Lukoki wrote a book called *The Purpose of Existence: How I discovered my purpose* which resonated with me on a personal level. In his book he wrote that your purpose is not to serve you, it is to serve others. I firmly believe this is true because every single person I train or mentor, when asked about their *why*, always give a similar response. Their purpose has nothing to do with them, it's about serving others.

I want to challenge you the next time you go to a property seminar to listen keenly to the speaker's story. Listen and analyse whether their dream is to serve others or themselves. Your WHY may change from time to time so always remain aware. Any shift in your why should be reflected and supported by your actions.

If I kept my light hidden or let the circumstances, I was going through lead me astray from my vision or path, I would not be the Napa I am today. I would possibly be playing football in some professional league and not serving the world. I was once so broken that I wanted to take my own life or rebel by hurting anyone who crossed my path, but I always wanted to run with big dogs, inspire and lead people to financial success. I believe employment and our current education system stifle or kill creativity by placing value on certain subjects and ignoring children who excel in areas not considered mainstream.

You have the potential to change the narrative society has constructed for you and write your own story. I want you to create your own legacy by becoming a leader in your field so you can let your own light shine. A single light in the darkness can bring hope to the hopeless.

Since 2015, I have not worked for anyone. I wanted to have the freedom of choice and rent-to-rent provided me with that option. I am forever grateful. Rent-to-rent gave me the opportunity to create other streams of income that I never thought of.

This simple strategy allowed me to create cashflow by controlling other people's assets. It allowed me to invest in a variety of business projects and gave me the opportunity to start a cleaning and maintenance business. It provided me with the time to pursue a childhood desire of becoming an author. My first book was an Amazon Best Seller. Rent-to-rent is no longer my only stream of income, but it is my starting point.

Success attracts success. At the height of my successful journey as a rent-to-rent property entrepreneur people started contacting me for help. Initially I gave out free advice and content. I was happy to help others to start their business journey. I never considered this as an income stream. Then in 2016 I went to a property event in Peterborough and before the keynote speaker went on stage a few people approached me and asked if I could mentor them. I did not feel as if I had the requisite skillset or the experience to teach people. Richard Branson once said, if you are offered an opportunity and you do not know what to do, say yes then go and learn how to do it. The keynote speaker asked me how many rent-to-rent properties I had in my portfolio and I told him. He then told me, if you can help a newbie from zero to the figure you just told me, then you can mentor. I left that event knowing I could be a mentor.

After leaving the event I wanted to gauge my skills and develop my confidence so one day I posted on a property group asking anyone who wanted help with their rent-to-rent business to meet me in Islington, Angel Starbucks. Surprisingly, many people showed up and I helped each one of them on a one to one basis. The following day my phone kept ringing. The people I had helped wanted to know how much I charged for my services.

Surprisingly, I did not have any paying package ready. I asked one person to call me in fifteen minutes then I quickly drafted a series of package I could offer. The majority went for the highest cost package and that is how my training and mentoring business started. Since then I have mentored many people to get their rent-to-rent deals and establish their businesses. Some of my mentees have now left their day jobs and doing rent-to-rent full-time.

The lyrics of Jay Z's song Moment of Clarity include the line, "I can't help the poor if I'm one of them." Therefore, I had to climb the ladder before I started pulling people up. Now I have trained people to leave their jobs and start creating multiple streams of income. Jeremiah 1vs5 states "before I created you in the womb, I knew you; before you were born, I set you apart". As a devout Christian, this is one of my favourite bible passages. It means my journey had already been written and it is my duty to find it and act. This verse consciously motivates me to do more to better myself because the higher I climb the more people I can help.

If I did not take any action you would not be reading this book. If I did not act, every agent, tenant and landlord I have worked with, would be impacted because of all the transactions and interactions that could only have occur through meeting me. Understanding this is very powerful. If you do not search to find your purpose and take appropriate actions, you are wasting your life. If you are not fulfilling your purpose, then you are blocking another person's opportunity to become successful.

Most people do not live according to their purpose due to lack of finance. They envision chasing their dreams and overnight the money will miraculously appear. They then become disaffected with the process when they realise, they must put some work into fulfilling their purpose.

I have always dreamt of becoming a public speaker, author, rapper and entrepreneur. As time passes, I am ticking off my accomplishments. My why is helping others and it gives me the drive to keep pushing. I want to leave a legacy that my children and others can be proud of. In my next book I will teach you the basics of *How to become the CEO of your life?*

You must let your light shine to inspire others to do the same. Whatever change you want to make in this world starts when you act.

I am now helping many outside the rent-to-rent industry with my experience and wisdom to improve their business using various strategies. I am also helping people that have money in the bank but earning paltry rates of interest to increase their money by investing in my projects.

I am now being invited to speak at numerous property events and I take my best performing students to share the stage with me. These experiences are exhilarating, and I feel like a proud father when I sit and watch my students sharing their journey in rent-to-rent. Human beings have a natural tendency to help others and when I asked my students how they found the experience;

the answers are always the same. We are grateful for the chance to live our dreams and help others in the process.

One of my mentees called Chun, whose journey is shared later in this book was humbled and elated I chose to give him a platform to share his story. His reception and feedback from the audience was amazing as his story resonated with many attendees.

Hopefully this chapter will ignite the light within you. A verse from Matthew 5 vs15 reminds us that people do not light a lamp and put it under a basket. Instead, put it on top of a lampstand, so that it shines on all who are in the house. Verse 16 admonishes us to let our light shine before people so that they can see the good things you do. My mentees recognised the importance of shining, they decided and acted upon it. Rent-to-rent is definitely not an easy property strategy or a get rich quick scheme but if it is done correctly, the cashflow you obtain can be life changing.

Chapter III

Global Pandemic

"In the middle of difficulty lies opportunity."
*– **Albert Einstein***

In early 2020 the world went on hold because of the outbreak of Coronavirus that originated in China. Up to the time this book was published no vaccine had been found. Contracting the virus could prove lethal. As deaths started to rise and the rate of infections gained momentum across the globe, the government decided the best option to protect the population was to send the nation into lockdown. The population was instructed to stay at home. If you had any known symptoms that was linked to the virus you had to self-isolate and remain in quarantine for a minimum period of fourteen days.

The pandemic threatened the world's economy and the majority of businesses had to shut down as employees were instructed not to return to work until further notice. Schools were closed, sports organisation such as the premier league and the NBA also postponed games; large events were forced to cancel or postpone. The world seemed like it was caught in a horror movie.

Most businesses were severely impaired, not excluding, the rent-to-rent and serviced accommodations which were heavily impacted, as most bookings were cancelled, and future bookings were under threat of cancellation. As a businessman you must always have a contingency plan and prepare for the inevitable. Granted no one could have predicted the outbreak of coronavirus nor the actions that followed, lessons can still be learned. The businesses that survive are the ones who learn valuable lessons during a crisis instead of throwing the towel at the first sign of trouble.

If we ever experience a recurrence of these circumstances, I have learned several lessons that could serve you well for future pandemics subject to it having similar effect and reactions.

1. Knowledge is Power: Quite often entrepreneurs avoid news platforms because of the negativity attributed to them. Total avoidance can however be fatal for any business. Key information is sometimes transmitted via these platforms and as I outlined in the chapter on Mamba attitude, speed of reaction is vital for success. If there are new developments that can negatively or positively affect your business, then knowledge is power. The government applied guidelines to keep everyone safe from contracting the virus or spreading it needed to be implemented in your business quickly. New measures were also introduced to support businesses and people affected by the virus.

2.   Mindset: I always talk about mindset because I understand how vital it is for success in life. In the initial stages of the pandemic you could almost feel people's fears and anxiety. People who were usually calm suddenly became stressed and started to panic. This is the expected results when you allow the external to influence the internal more that how the internal influences the external. This is a lesson best learnt early to help you weather any storms you may encounter both in your personal and professional life. When you are highly emotional it is difficult to reason and make logical and rational decisions.

3.   Keeping accurate records: A detailed record of tenants including the referencing report, their jobs and the company they work for can help you to take swift and decisive actions that could keep your business afloat. Good record keeping allows you to plan for the potential fallouts during a crisis. If your tenant is working for a company that shuts down, that could affect their ability to pay you rent. Being aware could help you mitigate your losses by applying for available grants or implementing a payment schedule for missed rent. Any property that is not performing as predicted is an indicator that it could be time to return it to the owner and focus on better performing

properties. Your focus should be on improving cash flow and the survival of your business.

4.   Open communication: During this period of hardship it is important to maintain an open dialogue with both tenants and the landlord. In a national crisis with everyone working together and supporting each other, it will make it easier to get through. By keeping an open communication channel, you can plan quickly.

5.   Opportunity: Warren Buffett once said, "We simply attempt to be fearful when others are greedy and to be greedy when others are fearful." In this moment, many people are fearful due to the uncertainty on the market. The measures enforced by the government saw more people remaining inside under quarantine. This meant that less people were viewing properties. I spoke with one of my agents who told me, "Napa, would you believe that the phone has not rang one single time before you called? You are the only person that has contacted us for viewings."

This pandemic affected the balance between supply and demand on the property market, as less people were viewing properties. This meant that the supply far exceeded the demand.

The selling market was also littered with opportunities. With the uncertainty of what may or may not happen, vendors became more motivated to sell. The mamba attitude should see you climbing to the treetops to spot opportunities. One of my mentees did just that.

Kyle Hart

My name is Kyle Hart and I come from a small town called Nantwich. As soon as I left school, I got an apprenticeship in engineering. The company I worked for was very supportive and helped me to progress quickly by paying the school fees so I could complete my HNC and HND in engineering. I loved my job because it did not feel like actual work.

However, when I got home from work each evening, I felt as if I was wasting my life. All I did each day was go to work, come home then sit on my phone for a few hours or maybe play on my PS4. I would then shower, go bed then repeat the cycle again and again. I felt like a hamster on a wheel, busily working but going nowhere fast.

One day I decided that I was going to use my spare time to learn something new. At this point I did not know what I wanted so I started searching on the internet and YouTube for ideas. I came across a video showing ways you can buy houses with no money.

This piqued my interest and I started watching more YouTube videos about property investing. I spent hours watching videos. I started attending some free property events on my own. My mum and dad would make jokes about me going to these events. However, I kept going and started to meet likeminded people. They started giving me recommendations for books, so I started reading.

I decided to really focus on rent-to-rent HMOs. This led to even more studying, reading and watching YouTube videos. At this point, I had a very good basic knowledge on rent-to-rent HMO's but didn't know how to take the next step. I then decided to get a mentor to help me start my property journey, ensure that I was fully compliant and help to guide me. This was one of the best decisions I ever made. I got mentored by Napa and he helped me with everything from setting up my company to making sure I was compliant. Each week we would have a video coaching session and set new goals for the week ahead. This really helped me to get started and keep focussed. With Napa's guidance I was able to secure two rent-to-rent six-bedroom HMO's bringing in a net profit £1532 per month. Everything was already set up and there were tenants in both properties. I was able to do this because the previous operator of the HMO's did not want to continue due to the uncertainty and risk from Coronavirus. I also understood the risks and the uncertainty about the upcoming months but instead of running, I factored this in when I negotiated the deal. I ensured that I put measures in place to protect myself and my tenants. The landlord and I had an open conversation and I agreed to take both of the properties if she was happy to work with us through these hard times. We agreed to review the rent on a month by month basis until the Coronavirus was no longer a threat. This meant that the landlord would be flexible about the rent if some months not all tenants could pay. This lowered my risk, and the landlord isn't at a loss as we agreed to set up a payment plan to make up for any rent reductions. This deal was truly a 'no money down' deal because I inherited the property from a previous rent-to-rent operator, I did not pay any fees or money towards anything.

Napa then called me one day and informed me that he knew a guy who was looking to get out of rent-to-rent due to the current situation. I saw this as my next big opportunity. I ensured that I had some money to give me security in the upcoming months to help with rent if needed. One of my biggest challenges was convincing the landlord that I was capable to take these properties as I am only twenty years old. She was shocked when I told her my age and I could see that she was doubtful. To overcome this, I explained that I am being mentored by someone that is experienced. The landlord also knew Napa which helped with my credibility. I demonstrated to the landlord that I had good knowledge of the area because I had already done my research. I learned early that it was important to know the area you want to invest in. This finally convinced her of my capability.

As both six bed HMO's were sourced directly from the landlords, I did not have to go through any references. I have had a deal stalled before due to referencing and to overcome this, I offered a guarantor. The upside with my new deals means that these landlords will now be able to provide references for me when I decide to expand my portfolio.

Both properties had one room empty in each. This was easily filled as I had already found people on Spare Room wanting rooms in those areas. I collected all the references from the previous operator to ensure all the tenants were good fits for the properties and were working professionals.

The management of the properties was a bit complicated at first because I had to issue new contracts to all tenants and also set up gas, electricity and water. However, once all these were in place it was easy to manage as I had good tenants in both properties.

The first few months we had to work with the tenants as many lost their jobs or was put on unpaid leave due to Covid19. We worked with the tenants and gave them a reduced rent, deferring the balance to be paid over the upcoming months. I enjoy managing both of the six bed properties as I am providing a roof over people's heads. The best moment for me was signing for the properties and then meeting all the tenants. I thoroughly enjoyed the whole process.

The best advice I would give to someone is, look for opportunities and when they come along grab them with both hands. If it was not for the Coronavirus outbreak, I would not have had the opportunity to take these properties as the previous operator was making good profit each month.

My top five giveaway tips would be:

- *Get as much free education as you can.*

- *Get a mentor. This helped me massively.*
- *Do not be scared to take a risk.*
- *Know the area you are operating in.*
- *Be patient, not all deals are good deals.*

After Brexit, the property market became very hot, with properties being purchased above the asking price. However, during the coronavirus pandemic, agents were contacting me, even on Sundays to offer properties. Vendors were becoming more flexible on negotiating prices. My mentees were all asking if it's a good time to acquire new properties. For me it is always a good time to take properties, but your negotiation skills have to be top class. You can take a property, but you have to bear in mind the current climate and negotiate terms that is acceptable and mutually beneficial to both parties.

6.   Contingency funds: Most people want to get involved in property investments to become financially independent and replace their jobs income. I always teach my mentees to set a specific figure that represents financial freedom and plan accordingly.

For example, if your figure is one thousand pounds per month and you secure a rent-to-rent deal with a cash flow of one thousand pounds per month then decide to quit your job, that is a risky manoeuvre. When you extract one thousand pounds from your business, you make yourself a thousand pounds richer, but your business is now a thousand pounds poorer.

Your business will always need extra funding to cover unexpected costs such as maintenance or accidental breakages. You would not be able to pay those bills if you already took all the money out of the business. Most people recommend saving ten percent of your profits for any contingency that may arise. I believe that is not enough. I teach my mentees to keep fifty percent of their net profit for contingencies. This ensure you will always have enough funds in your business to cover any unexpected costs.

7.   Exit plan: You must always have an exit plan in place to protect you from losing money. The beauty about rent-to-rent is that we do not own these properties, we only control them. Therefore, it gives us the flexibility to return the property if it is not performing subject to contract. In securing any property, always make sure you have clauses in your agreement with the landlord that allows you to exit without any excessive costs.

When you are making your business plan you should put clauses and caveats in place that will protect you from periods like this. For many people this may be their first time experiencing a pandemic on this scale, and many businesses will suffer financial losses, but it will give us some invaluable lessons in resilience and perseverance. Undoubtedly the experience gained should help us plan for the future.

Chapter IV

Sales & Marketing

"There is no sale without the story; no knockout without the setup."
— Gary Vaynerchuk

Sales and marketing are the lifeline of most businesses, yet it is quite often neglected or treated as a secondary appendage to the business. Most entrepreneurs when they embark on their journey leave this aspect of their business to chance. This area, in my opinion is quite often overlooked in most rent-to-rent training. I have therefore dedicated an entire chapter with the help of a friend to teach you some rudimentary skills when it comes to sales and marketing.

I once read that the average millionaire has at least seven different streams of income. I took that idea and applied to many aspects of my business including sales and marketing. If you apply the idea of multiplicity to your marketing strategy and have seven instead of only two ways of sourcing property deal i.e. calling agents or sending mails, then you have maximised the chances of your business gaining the attention you need.

Imagine having more than seven ways of contacting agents or landlords to secure a property deal, that would increase your probability of success drastically. For most people Spare Room is the only platform they use to source tenants. This over reliance on one source means that you are totally dependent on the traffic passing through this platform to get your property tenanted. Any unrelated issues involving Spare Room could harm your business beyond repair. A technical malfunction on the website directly affects your business because you have no control over this third part website. If you do not have alternatives or back up media to disseminate marketing materials, then you will struggle.

You need to research different platforms and spaces that could provide you with tenants. It is a much better position when you have too many tenants to choose from than very little. Tenants can be sourced from various platforms.

For example, in one of our property we built a great relationship with an Amazon international recruiter. His job involved recruiting Amazon delivery drivers from eastern European countries and employ them here in the UK. We became his first point of contact for any accommodation need. Once he recruited an employee, we would then provide the accommodation.

Another case involved building a relationship with a letting agent in the area, and they found us tenants. We still conducted our own due diligence on tenants and if the prospective tenant passed, we then accommodate them.

Sales is the blood of every business. Business relies on sales. Without a doubt the greatest skill you can possess is being able to sell. It is a skill that we use every day without any thought. We dress a certain way because subconsciously we are selling ourselves. We sell ourselves at interviews, in conversations and in business. Selling is a mindset. In the rent-to-rent business, selling is fundamental. If you cannot close a deal, you are doomed for failure.

Your business should be based on fair exchange; where you provide a product or service and get paid for it. Many people fail to close a sale or use proven sales techniques while conducting viewings with their potential tenants. If you have already done the hard work of getting them into your property, you must know how to close the deal and get them to sign on the dotted line.

Do not sell the room, sell the benefits they get from living there. The kitchen is not just a room with appliances, it is where great meals are created and shared with good friends. Allow your tenants to use their imaginations and see what it will be like when they move in. Talk about the distance to the local amenities and why it is a positive. Sell! Sell! Sell!

Remember to pause and allow your prospective tenants time to think. Do not overload them with information or rush them into signing. Most people tend to be turned off if they feel pressured to commit. Ask open ended questions like, what are you looking for in a property? How do you feel about the house? Listen carefully to their responses. Build on positive responses and address any concerns they voice. If they compliment the size of the bedroom, then agree and share how many pieces of furniture could fit into the room leaving enough space to enjoy. If they complain about light coming into the room, explain how the use of mirrors strategically placed will brighten up the room immensely.

Incorporate personal stories where possible that triggers an emotional response. Maya Angelou once said, 'People may forget what you say or what you do, but they will never forget how you made them feel'.

This chapter is written by Mitesh Parmar, who spent most of his career in the cooperate world working as a global product manager, his career was spent across multiple industries from food manufacturing, x-ray machine for electronics, SaaS software and the rail sector.

Mitesh has launched products globally, trained sales professional, presented to large audiences and worked in marketing and sales capacity when developing and launching products.

He's got a BEng degree in Electronics & Software engineering, qualification in marketing from the Charted Institution of Marketing and Diploma in Training which has allowed Mitesh to easily communicate complicated engineering solutions to the market and vice versa when selling and launching products/services.

Mitesh also spent his time volunteering and supporting the Birmingham tech community. Today Mitesh uses his transferable skills in the property sector while providing marketing consultancy, running a startup architect firm and property business in the Midlands. Even though Mitesh does not do rent to rent, he was asked to part some of his knowledge and experience in the field of marketing and sales. In addition, he also loves Pizza!

"It's not what you do, it's WHY you do it"

– Mitesh Parmar

Due to the depth of the topics to cover, I will cover them in brief with references which will allow you to dive deeper. No point re-inventing the wheel, right? I'm no expert and nor claim to be, I'm merely giving pointers where you can go and learn more. In addition, I'm sharing tips I wish someone had told me many years ago. Please use this information with caution and do your own research. I will not be held responsible for any of your actions. Always be responsible, ethical and have morals, it is what sets humans apart from other species. Let's crack on…

1.   Marketing

Marketing and sales are two interesting topics, and both are very much interlinked however serve different purposes. I'll start with marketing, as marketing is the first process of any business. When I was an engineer and moved into a sales development and eventually a product manager role, one colleague once said to me "so now you are going to be doing fluffy brochures", oh boy was he wrong. You see, most understand marketing as what you see, datasheets, ads, flyers, however marketing is much, more than this.

Take this quote below for the definition of marketing.

"The management process responsible for identifying, anticipating and satisfying customer requirements profitably"

-*Charted Institute of Marketing*

Marketing is about understanding the **CHALLENGES** your target audience faces, then providing a solution. At the same time understanding all the micro (small factors you can control) and macro (larger aspects) environments which can impact the delivery of this product/service.

A classic example here is the story of Henry Ford who built the Ford motor vehicle. When he asked the market what they wanted at the time, they all said, "A faster horse", he knew they wanted to get from A to B quicker, so he made the first car. He truly understood the market needs and challenges and delivered a solution. In the modern world, this is similar to Steve Jobs and the first iPhone or tablet (Even though Microsoft made the first tablet, the timing and implementation were not right, but that's me going off-topic!) Steve understood the challenges.

WHY?

With the above in mind and as we continue the big question in the property business is to understand your WHY?, as this ultimately will help you stand out in your rent-to-rent business and will help you push through the challenges you face in your business.

Simon Sinek explains this well in his book "Start with Why", he has a great YouTube video on this, search for Start with Why, it's a TED talk with over 6 million views, and has put a lot of content out there about this. Let me take this moment to fill you in a bit.

The Golden Circle

WHAT

Everyone knows WHAT they do

HOW

Some know HOW they do it. The process which makes you unique

WHY

Very few know WHY they do what they do. WHY does your business exist in the first place?

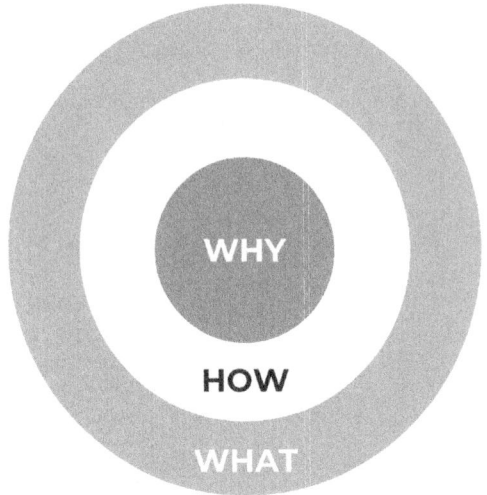

What Simon explains is that most businesses pitch WHAT they do, HOW they do it, then WHY they do it, working their way from the outside in. Where it should be from the inside out. Why are you doing what you do, then how you do it, then what you are doing.

If you are doing rent-to-rent and speaking to landlords then what is your WHY, how are you different to everyone else, what's your purpose? Once you figure this out, it will make communicating your message via marketing much easier and will help build empathy and rapport with the landlord. You can find an example of my why at the end of this chapter.

I think naturally for most it is financial freedom, however, think if you had all the money what would you do, who would you help, what would you do next? You can then focus on this instead of just money.

Now remember this is not just about you, it is about the landlord. Understanding YOUR why is important as you start the journey as it will keep you going and make your messaging clearer.

"Working hard for something we don't care about is called stress: Working hard for something we love is called passion."

— Simon Sinek

Five WHYs

Now to move onto the landlords WHY. As I said from the beginning, marketing and business are about solving a problem. If you can solve a problem, you can sell a product/service. Amazon, Uber, Air B&B all solve a problem, from saving time to convenience. When offering a rent-to-rent service, you are like many others, of course, you'd be offering guaranteed rent as one key benefit, plus a few others. However, what does that mean to the landlord? Why is that so important to THEM?

Fives whys was developed by Toyota, the car manufacturing giant. It is used as part of route cause analysis. It is acting like a child asking "Why" several times to an answer, to help dig deeper in the real meaning behind the problem.

Take the example below;

Problem: run through a red light

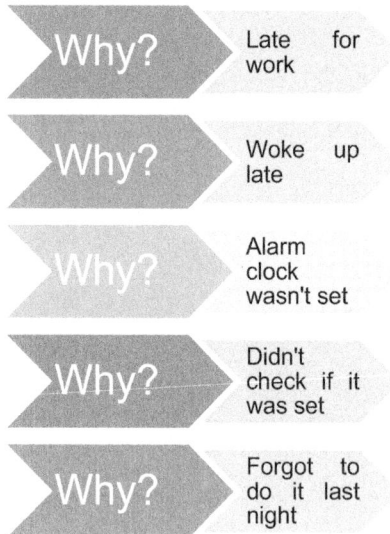

Why?	Late for work
Why?	Woke up late
Why?	Alarm clock wasn't set
Why?	Didn't check if it was set
Why?	Forgot to do it last night

Solution: Set a reminder to check the alarm clock.

It's a crude example, however, it illustrates the point that asking "why" several times helps to dig deeper. This can also be applied in everyday life to understand underlying issues and problem.

When speaking to someone who wants to sell a property or even get you to manage it could go something like this;

What challenges are you having with renting your property?

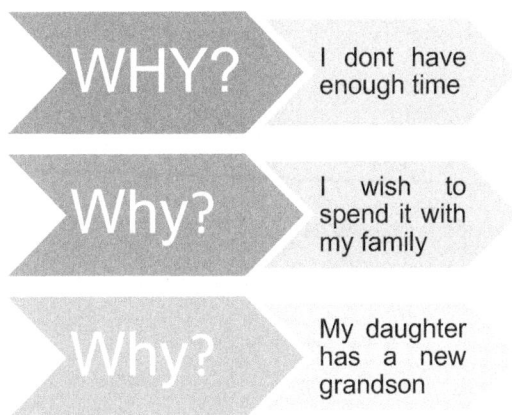

WHY?	I dont have enough time
Why?	I wish to spend it with my family
Why?	My daughter has a new grandson

Now in this example we only needed to go 3 levels deep, sometimes you may need to go further. Here the landlords' true motive is that they want to spend time with their grandchild. Now, what if when you are talking to them you focused your solution on time management and relayed back how they would feel spending time with their grandson? Sounds like a great proposition, right? On the other hand, if you focused on yourself and just continued with your typical textbook speech, would that have worked? Maybe, maybe not.

In this case, you need to understand their pain points and how you can help them. This is why it's important to understand their true WHY and the five why technic helps with this. Like any business, this is a business and not a strategy, treat clients with respects, do what you say you will do, be honest and really help them. Get proper understanding and learn the pros and cons before going in deeper.

Kotlers Product Level

Philip Kotler, a marketing and economist said that for a product to sell it needs to satisfy **needs**, **wants** and **demands**, it has to have more value than something tangible. He developed five product models. These levels attach themselves to the level of value you can get.

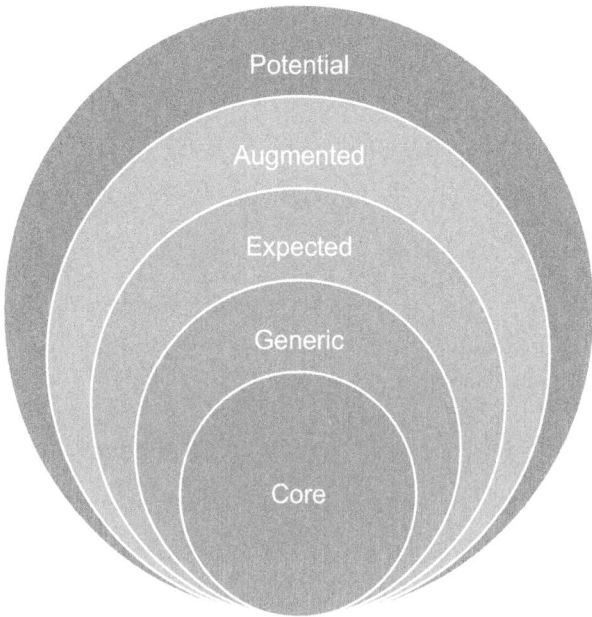

Core

This is the fundamental of what the product has to perform. For example, a warm coat will protect you from rain and wind. For rent-to-rent this could be guaranteed rent, as this is the basic need.

Generic

This is about the qualities, i.e. material, fit, quality of zips. For rent-to-rent this could be a 3-year contract, new furniture etc. Its additional qualities which support the core product offering.

Expected

This is what the customer expected. In the coat example, its being really warm, being comfortable, look good. In rent-to-rent, they expect you to be a limited company, be professional, trustworthy, deliver on your promise.

Augmented

This is where you have the opportunity to stand out from the competition. Here are features and benefits which sets you apart. For rent-to-rent what can you offer that adds value, what sets you apart? Keep the furniture after the term? Experience? Working with an established partner/mentor? Local knowledge? Desire and hungry to succeed? Working full time in property?

Potential

This is what can happen in the future. What changes your product/service can undergo to add more value. For example, a warm coat that is thin and light as a feather with a new coating. This is more about your future product/service offerings, this shows to the customer that you will have something new and they wish to work with you. For rent-to-rent you could consider favourable extension terms, re-decorate etc.

Kotler's model highlights that people expect more than the norm, and this is what they buy. People buy "wants" not "needs", i.e. you **need** a jumper to keep you warm, but you **want** a designer jumper to impress your friends, so you feel good. Like a car, you **need** a car to get you from A to B, any car will do this, but you **want** a nice fancy car to feel good about yourself.

7P's

This is another classic marketing tool used in business. The 7Ps represents seven core elements on your product/service. Originally this was the 4Ps. Each element goes into a deeper context, I'll focus on a few. You should be able to research the rest.

Promotion

Promotion is about getting your message out there to the right people, at the right time. There are various forms you can use;

- Identity

- Meaning

- Feeling

- Values

- Mission

- Ethics

How they feel when they think of you

Consider when doing your branding what you want other to feel. The use of colours (Google 'colour meaning'), typography, style and wording all have an impact. Are you going for a professional company, easy-going, fun, natural, calm, etc.

Try to avoid making lots of different colour options and then asking other people what they think, it's your business, it's what you represent. Of course, get different version and colour gradients to get feedback, however, avoid making a green one, red one, blue one than asking for feedback. You will never please everyone and like most things, it will be subjective.

Touchpoints

I just wanted to touch on 'touchpoints' (pun intended). In most sales cycle, it is very rare for someone to buy a product straight away. People want to learn, trust and get to know your business. Typically, it takes someone 7 touchpoints before they buy a product. This could be seeing an ad, speaking with you, flyer etc. So, the point I'm making here is you need to keep pushing your messaging. These days most of this is online. Let's use Napa's mentoring program as an example. Many people that contacts Napa for his mentoring program would of have touchpoints from his YouTube channel, Instagram contents, word of mouth from current or previous mentees, his book, events his speaks at etc but his message and mission is circulating on what he offers.

Sales / Business

Value Proposition Canvas

The value proposition canvas was developed by the team at https://www.strategyzer.com/ and was the second instalment after the Business Model Canvas. This is a great model used by many businesses globally from large organisations to start-ups. There are tonnes of information online on how to use this along with the book from the authors. I'll take a moment to explain why this applies to rent-to-rent and your business.

The value proposition canvas takes into account two important segments from the business model canvas. One is focused on the customer segment and the Job-To-Be-Done framework and the other is the value proposition segment you are offering. If you get the two right and meet in the middle, you get product-market fit, also known as solving a challenge that someone will pay for.

Jobs to be done

Jobs to be done (JTBD) was a framework developed by Clayton Christensen a Harvard Business school professor. In simple terms, it was about understanding what job the customer was trying to get done. He has a great example with the McDonalds milkshake. In short, customers bought a milkshake because they wanted something to hold in their hand while driving so, they didn't want to fall asleep and also have it as breakfast. Understanding this allowed McDonalds to better position their marketing message.

I suggest using this model, along with the five why's, to understand the job the landlord is trying to get done.

Gains / Pains

Do further reading to get a better understanding of this. But in short, when doing the Job, it will create pains, what you don't want and gains, what you do want.

Work on your value and consider how you will solve the pain, gains and JTBD.

The Value Proposition Canvas

Value Proposition

Customer Segment

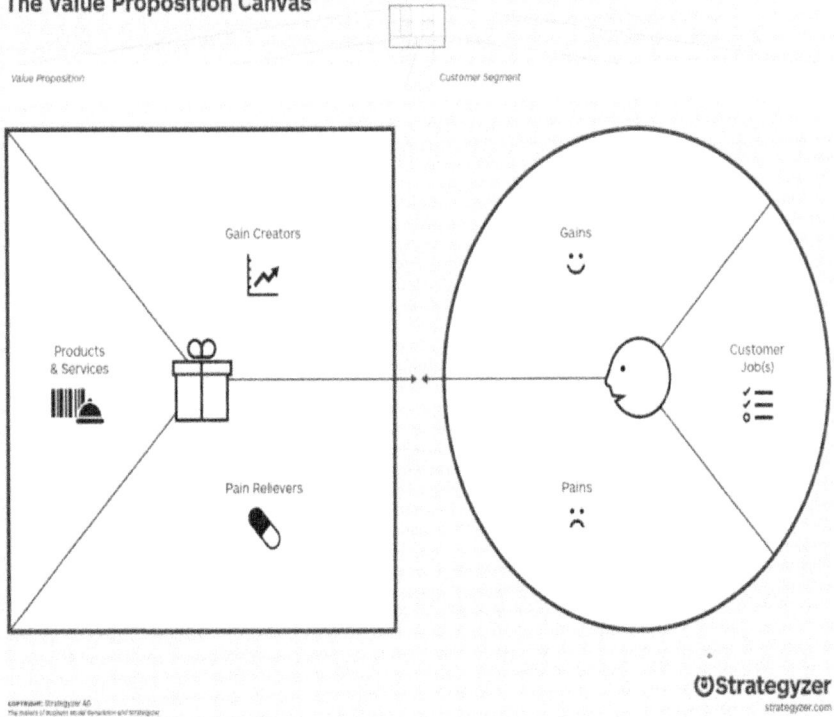

Gain Creators

Gains

Products & Services

Pain Relievers

Customer Job(s)

Pains

©Strategyzer
strategyzer.com

For example, a landlord wants passive income, the gain could be more time with the family, pain could be little experience in interior design and keeping up with modern trends. Your solution could be to offer them the time back, via your experience.

When you read up more on this, you will find there are multiple options using this.

Business Model Canvas

This is where it all started for the Strategyzer team. Again, plenty of information on the web about this. This is more related to the wider business strategy and is useful to run your business, I feel many start-ups can benefit from learning about this model as it gives a very good holistic approach to business.

The Business Model Canvas

Communication

Communication, communication, communication…. Every day we communicate, it is how we live, work, love and laugh. It's a vital skill to have.

There are generally three main methods of communicating, words (written text), aural (spoken words), visual (body language). Now, I am sure you are all aware the visual communication is the most effective. You can tell how someone feels before they even say anything.

Followed by aural, when talking on the phone your tempo, speed, rhythm and quality all make an impact on how the other person understands this.

Written words in an email or letter are the least effective as its very hard to put across emotion and build empathy.

Therefore, it's important not to sell over the phone or in a letter. The job of a phone call or letter is to get a face to face meeting. This is true for most sales, especially if it is a cold call.

Tip: If calling someone, its best to stand up and talk. Standing up opens your diaphragm and allows you to talk more naturally. Also, stand with your chest out and head up.

This will help build confidence in your delivery. Try it, you will be amazed at the small difference this can make.

Words to use

Subtle differences in the words we use can tell you a lot about a person, take this example,

"Did you hear about the new building opening?"

"Did you see the new building opening?"

"How do you feel about the new building opening?"

The end results are the same, it is asking someone about their thoughts on a new building. However, you can tell that one person is more of an auditory person, one is more visually and the last is emotional. In our case, we always want to focus on the emotionally side, as I said before people buy with emotion. Your emotional side of the brain decides it wants something and then your logical side tries to justify it. Therefore, when in sales it is always best to use words which engages the emotional side.

Mirroring

Mirroring is a classic sales technic used to build on the adage of people buy from people like themselves. You like and trust someone who has similar values to you. A method to do this is to mirror their behaviour (action and speech). This once again helps to build rapport and trust. Please be ethical and not take advantage. I won't go into detail here, however, research mirroring and there will be lots of information and resource out there for you. This will help you with your sales.

Framing

This sales technic is based on framing questions to help the path of the answer. A classic is… "What did you like about this?" This assumes they liked something and pushes the path down a positive answer. (Not so good if you are using it for research, you would be better of saying "how did you feel about this?")

Framing questions or statements are also useful to head off any objections that you know you will get. For example, is property is in a noisy location you could say "this property comes with triple-glazed windows" while doing the viewing. What this does, is it stops any negative thoughts in their mind and moves them onto something else. Otherwise, they would be playing out negative scenarios in their head about staying awake at night, not being to get up for work, etc.

Stories

My final tip is 'Stories', stories always sell. Everyone remembers a story. If you want someone to remember what you have said tell them a good story. A great example of this is a book called The Alchemist by Paulo Coelho, it's a powerful message told via a story – a must-read.

"There is one thing that makes a dream impossible to achieve: the fear of failure"

- ***Paulo Coelho***

In rent-to-rent you can use this when trying to explain how you can help, maybe give them an example of another landlord and their situation before you came to help. Instead of saying "I helped a landlord with xyz", you can say "I help David from Midlands, he was fed with late payments, I've had his property for 14 months now, and his so happy that he can spend time with his grandkids, he recently went to Wales with them". Now, which one would you remember? The main reason here is that fact that you can visualise the story in our brain and therefore remember it more.

Stories sell, always tell great stories. But don't lie or miss lead.

My Why

1 in 4 people suffer from mental health issues. 1 in 5 show signs of anxiety and depression. Research shows one contributing factor is the environment we are in. We spend 90% of our time indoors and 65% is in our own homes. The population is set to grow by 10% over the next 15 years. The country needs over 300,000 new homes **EVERY YEAR!** The existing building stock is not designed with people's health and wellbeing in mind. There are many people not happy and much of the population suffering from stress and anxiety that can lead to chronic health conditions, which is having an impact on the NHS and on productivity. Pollution and toxins from manmade products are increasing adding to poor health conditions as well as the impact on the climate.

I am the co-founder of Wellspace Properties and our sister company Wellspace Architects. Working alongside my wife who is a charted Architect, we are on a mission to create happier and healthier lives through sustainable human-centric developments and design.

Summary

Marketing is about understanding the challenge you are trying to solve, communicating this effectively and delivering a great service. Sales are helping the prospect through their journey and supporting them with any questions and getting the value exchange across the line.

It must be a win-win and work both ways.

I hope you found this information useful and should give you some direction to go and dig deeper.

Remember to treat this as a business, add value and most of all make a difference for good in the world, this is your opportunity.

I also wanted to take this opportunity to say a massive thank you to Napa for allowing me to help others. Many thanks Napa, you are very humble, and it has been great working with you!

If anyone wants to connect with me you can find me on Facebook, LinkedIn, Twitter and Instagram, or email me at hello@wellspaceproperties.com or hello@wellspacearchitects.com

Chapter V

Real Life Experiences

"Change is our chance to experience the new, to identify additional options and generate different opportunities" - **Barbara Lucas**

In this chapter I asked my mentees to share their experiences with rent-to-rent. I believe in keeping everything real, therefore you will know the highs and lows that each mentee went through while building their rent-to-rent business. The idea behind this chapter is to give you an insight into the multiplicity of backgrounds, ethnicity, geographical locations and entry points into the rent-to-rent business. This is not a business for the fainthearted. Similar to *The Rent to Rent Blueprint* this will give you a very in depth, detailed and relatable overview which I believe will give more value.

Carol Mbaya

My name is Carol Mbaya. I am a mother to an amazing one year old. I was born in Zimbabwe and came to the UK at the age of eleven. I did my SAT's, GCSE's and then went to college to study for a BTEC in Business Studies. From a very young age I always wanted to have my own business that would enable me to help others and become an inspiration to young people. During my GCSE's and college years I began to run my own mobile hairdressing business but after a couple of years I got bored of it. After College I decide to go to university to study for a degree in Criminological and Forensic Psychology, however, my passion for business and helping young people was still there. In late 2014, I decided to register a community interest company that works with youth offenders and ex-youth offenders, helping them to realise their potential whether through education, starting their own business or getting a job.

My property journey was inspired by my grandad who passed away when I was five years old. I remember growing up with my dad and he would share with me how my grandad had a lot of commercial and residential properties in Zimbabwe. He would use some of the proceeds from these assets to help people in need in his village and community. This really resonated with me and fuelled my desire for property investment as a way to fund the projects that I would like to do with my community interest company as well as have investments of my own. In 2015, I began my journey by attending free property investments courses to gain knowledge in property investing and the best way to raise investment for properties. From these courses I heard about deal sourcing and lease options. That became my focus and strategy. I thought to myself, I have to find a mentor and get myself onto a mentorship program.

My journey to find a mentor was not easy. The first mentor that I found was through Facebook. To be honest I reasoned with myself, that this mentor was a woman who was making it in the property industry which really motivated me, so I thought "yep I want her to be my mentor". I joined her one-year online mentorship programme. The mistake I made was that I did not fully understand or researched the type of mentorship the mentor provided. It was not until I was on the programme that I realised most of the people on the programme were investors who already had huge portfolios of properties and I was a newbie in property investment with no portfolio or funds.

A year went by and I came out of the programme with no deals sourced or finance raised. I never blamed my mentor for this because if I had done my research, I would have known which mentor I should have chosen.

A couple months later I learnt about the rent-to-rent strategy through Facebook. I started reading and watched many videos about it. I then decided that I was going to focus on this strategy and make it work. With so many mentors out there, I faced another challenge.

Many people were now doing rent-to-rent, so it was difficult to find a mentor who was authentic, who understood your goals, vision and who wanted to see you win, not because it makes them credible but because they genuinely want to see you succeed. After a lot of soul searching and prayers, I finally found a mentor (Napa Bafikele) who was willing to spend time with me and shared everything that he knew about rent-to-rent.

I believe that you should run a business that you love and enjoy doing 24/7. Having a mentor has made my property journey more enjoyable. Having a mentor has helped me to grow into a leader. Having a mentor meant that I had someone that I was accountable to which meant that there was no slacking or procrastinating which is one of the major things that makes entrepreneurs fail.

My mentor also helped me in setting up a company and making it all compliant which is something that I did not get from my previous mentor. He also helped me to understand how to run a compliant rent-to-rent business and all the laws around compliancy. Having a mentor who encouraged and supported me allowed me to acquire three rent-to-rent properties in less than thirty days.

My first deal was found on Open Rent and I negotiated directly with the landlord. This was the first viewing I did and managed to secure a deal with a net profit of £795 per month. The landlord had never let his property to a company before, so I had to sit down with the landlord and explain how the business model worked and who was our clientele. I also gave him our offer and within an hour of viewing the property the landlord called me back and accepted my offer. The property is a four-bed maisonette with two bathrooms, a kitchen and a communal area.

The entry cost to the deal was £1300 for the first month of rent and £1500 for the deposit. I had some money saved up from my full-time job as an Executive Officer which I used to pay the upfront costs. The property came fully furnished and it was immaculately decorated because it was previously operated as a serviced accommodation.

The main challenge I faced was my own self-confidence. This was my first viewing where I had to convince a landlord to handover the keys to his property to a young girl who was just starting a business and having no experience. The support and encouragement from my mentor really helped me as he believed in me. He reminded me that nothing in life will be handed to me, I had to work for it.

After securing the deal, we advertised on Spare Room and Gumtree and managed to secure tenants who were working professionals. As this was my first deal, I was learning on the go. It was a steep learning curve. I had to change my mindset from someone who got things sold to them to becoming a salesperson. I had to quickly learn how to sell a room. Fortunately, the location of the property made it easy to get viewings as it was located next to the city centre. The flats used to be council flats and they still had this archaic style which turned off a few prospective tenants when they came to view. It gave them the impression that the area was rough which was not the case. To overcome this minor problem, we had to sell the benefits of the city location and explain that the flats were once run by the council but now they were not.

Managing tenants for the first time was a real struggle. As I was new to the game, I neglected to figure out the potential dynamics when strangers reside in a communal setting. Having people living together with different personalities under one roof can be a disaster waiting to happen. We had one particular tenant who had a lot of personal belongings which became a problem for the other tenants as their space was being encroached on. This became an ongoing problem and we lost two tenants in one week. We quickly realised that we had to do something, so we sat down and spoke to the tenants who were left and asked them to respect each other's space. We also helped by allocating cabinets for each tenant. We created a folder with the house rules that all tenants had to read and sign. We managed to quickly replace the tenants that moved out and all the tenants have been in the property now for more than six months.

I found the second property on Rightmove that is cash flowing a net profit of £1215 per month. After my viewing, I sent through an offer and it was accepted. This deal was pretty straight forward as the estate agent had heard of company let before and so it was easy to sell the concept to the landlord. This was a newly refurbished five-bedroom HMO with a conservatory, two receptions and three bathrooms, one being an en-suite.

The entry cost for the second property was £1600 for the first month's rent and £1800 for the deposit. The funding for this deal was a loan from a family member which allowed us to get all the basic furnishings for the property. Getting the property ready was fun as I am naturally quite creative, and it gave me a chance to combine business with a little pleasure. We also learned the new skill of haggling in order to get a bargain so that we got some great deals on furniture. Within a couple of days, we found three tenants who promptly moved in.

A few weeks later the property was fully tenanted, and all our tenants came from Spare Room. This time we learned lessons from the first property and made sure that all tenants were in the same age range and had similar interests.

Having dealt with the issue of tenant dynamics we encountered another issue in this property. While conducting an inventory check, we noticed a stain from a leak on one of the ceilings. We reported this to the estate agent immediately. It transpired that the company employed by the landlord to refurbish the property did not carry out the plumbing work properly. A lot of pipes where not connected which was resulted in blockages in the showers and toilets. Luckily, we noticed this early into the tenancy, so the landlord used his insurance to get it fixed. I was afraid that the tenants would move out or complain but because we were honest and handled the situation professionally, we built up a good rapport with both the tenants and the estate agent. The way we handled the emergency in our second property led to our third deal from the same agency.

This deal was an eight-bedroom HMO, with three bathrooms, one of which was en-suite, a living room and a kitchen. This is my highest cash flowing deal with a whooping £2,288 net profit per month.

The estate agent that we had been working with, asked if I would be interested in an eight-bedroom HMO which one of their landlords was looking to sell. I jumped at the idea and quickly asked for a viewing. I took the lessons learnt from the previous two properties that I had viewed and checked for any potential problems in the property. I noticed once again that one of the ceilings was leaking. I asked if this would be fixed before we take the property and the agent and landlord agreed. I felt hesitant taking on another property so soon as I felt I may be taking on too much too quickly and may struggle to manage it all.

The fear of success also overwhelmed me, and I started to second guess myself. I spoke to a friend, Richie, whom I knew through Napa's mentorship programme. Richie encouraged me and convinced me to put through an offer. I did and my offer was accepted. I was growing in confidence and managed to negotiate no first month's rent and no deposit. The only thing we had to pay was the flatfair which is similar to a deposit insurance and that was only £300. This property came unfurnished. As I did not have any funding, I joint ventured with my mentor Napa Bafikele and he provided the finance for all the basic furniture which was less than £3000.

The property was decorated and dressed by Milvia Serra. Once we had completed all the preparations, we noticed that there was still a leak on the ceiling that was supposed to have been fixed. I reported this to the estate agency again and was dragged through a long process to get this sorted. It took three months before it was finally sorted. From past experiences I made sure that the property was not tenanted until this was fixed. We wanted to make sure that our tenants moved into a fully prepared house, not one that would cause them undue stress and potentially affect our credibility later.

We also agreed with the estate agent that we would not pay any rent until this was sorted. This was a stressful period for me but having a mentor and a good relationship with the estate agent made it easy to overcome this challenge. We made sure we always kept the communication channels open.

The next challenge was getting tenants during the low season. This was just after Christmas and New Year's and not a lot of people were looking for places to stay or relocate; neither were they looking for jobs. This was not a variable I had factored into my plans. I had not thought about it nor had I heard anyone speak about the quiet season before we got the property. In life we are told to seize every moment and grab every opportunity, however you must also ensure the time is right. Every cloud has a silver lining. The delays in completing the repairs on the property gave us the time to look for the right tenants for the property.

My experience in managing HMO properties has been mostly rewarding although sometimes it brought me anxiety. There were times that I felt sick to my stomach when I got any phone call from a tenant. I kept thinking, what has happened now? Most times it was not as bad as I thought. I have really enjoyed building relationships with both the tenants, landlords and estate agents. I once naively thought running HMO's would be easy, but I can tell you honestly, it is not a walk in the park. There were times that I had to take my son to viewings and spend days and nights with him at the property trying to get it ready, but in the end, it has all been worth it.

My advice to anyone starting their business is make sure you know what you are getting yourself into. Make sure that you are willing to work hard. Tackle every challenge as it comes and do not try and get ahead of yourself as it can become overwhelming. Surround yourself with likeminded people because it can be a very lonely journey. You will feel discouraged and feel like giving up some days but when you have a good support system of people who motivate you and remind you of your worth, you can easily pick yourself up and go to face your challenges. Do not be driven only by money because the moment you are not making any profit you will easily become disaffected.

Chun – Eu Man

My name is Chun Eu Man and I live in Brighton. I work full time as a medical assessor. I have worked in over fifteen different roles in my life and just could not find a job that I could one hundred percent settle on. I kept thinking throughout my life about my family, how they started their own business and never worked for anyone. They became successful through hard work and being their own boss.

I thought my life was worth more than just working for a company. I wanted more freedom to make more money, be my own boss and be in a position to adequately care for my family and fiancée. I wanted my family to know that I could comfortably look after them and also make my fiancée the happiest girl in the world, enjoying life and not stressing about working for someone else. Life is more than just working; life is about taking risks and enjoying the ride, knowing that at the end of the journey it will all be worth it.

My first deal was in Portsmouth, I was trying to find deals in Brighton, but it was very difficult, so after three months Napa suggested to look for another area. Within a week of changing my area I found a deal. It was a five bedrooms property with three years agreement, the net profit was £640.

Networking and building relationships are key to getting more deals. A week after my first property in Portsmouth was fully tenanted, I managed to secure a second deal in Brighton through an estate agent. This deal cash flow was significantly higher than my first deal, after all expenses I was taking home a net profit of £950 per month.

I attended many investor events and stumbled across one of Napa's video explaining how he helped people to secure rent-to-rent deals. At first, I was sceptical because there are pros and cons when doing rent-to-rent and many mentors do not dwell on the cons. I decided to call Napa to get a better understanding of what he offered. His story about starting from nothing and getting to where he is now, impressed me. I realised that anything is possible through hard work. I wanted to leave a legacy that I worked hard to achieve and take the risk to provide for my family. I wanted to help people and I knew staying in my current job would not give me any satisfaction. I believe God created me to go out and help people change their lives. So, I took that leap of faith.

The mentorship with Napa provided the following; all the resources to get started, negotiating skills and techniques, contracts, strategies for finding deals and managing my portfolio. People are misguided if they think starting a property business without training will work. There is so much to learn to minimise risks and start on a solid foundation. I would have definitely failed if I did not do this mentorship. Anything is possible when you have a mentor that will push you in the right direction and help you physically and mentally.

Both deals were sourced via letting agents using Napa's guidance on how to speak with agents. The mentorship package I choose from Napa included a visit to my area. I requested him to accompany me as we viewed properties and spoke with several agents in the area. For my first deal I did not have the funds to finance it, so Napa introduced me to his other mentee that had cash but was time poor. Napa's other mentee provided the finance and acted as a guarantor and I managed to secure the deal and split the profit equally once his capital investment was paid back.

For my second deal, I had the funds to secure the property, but I did not have a guarantor. As I had built a good relationship with my joint venture partner from the first property, I offered him a percentage of the profit to act as a guarantor.

I faced many challenges, but I had to be patient and mentally resilient to push through. Property investments can be quite frustrating at times. I had a lot of upfront costs and I had to ruthlessly negotiate rent free terms and more. My recommendation is to always have an investor or a friend to listen to your worries and concerns without judgement or negative advice. Being an entrepreneur can be lonely and stressful. I learnt that I didn't need to bear all the burden alone through networking with other investors. I can guarantee you; they have gone through similar situations or worse.

Struggles can impair your mental health. Being your own boss requires a lot of patience and faith in seeing the bright side of problems. When you worry needlessly or want results now, your mental health can spiral out of control and leave you with many sleepless nights

I pushed through because I knew if I stopped, I would fail. Failure is not a sign weakness; failure is an opportunity that you can improve and keep going. I called Napa several times and he just said to me "If you can't get pass your worries, you might as well give up!" Now people might feel that this is harsh, but in reality, Napa was being honest. We live in a world where mentors just tell you "You can do this, you will be fine, just keep going". However, when Napa said that, I remember sitting in my car at ten o' clock one night saying to myself "I have already paid him! I can't just give up! I will prove to myself that I can do this!". I went at it and I did it. I got the deals and got all the rooms filled.

There are many obstacles and struggles to get a viewing on a property. Estate agents or landlord can reject your offer as it is too low. Trying to secure contracts, refurbishing the place as soon as possible can sometimes pose a problem. Finding the right tenants or waiting for potential tenants to click on your ads and message you, in some cases be an uphill task. Tenants being unhappy because it is cold, and the boiler is not working. Noisy next-door neighbour and the list goes on. Tenants sometimes have no feelings and just want you to get it done. You will soon understand when to stand your ground. Other times you have to be resilient in the business world and the meaning of "your word is your bond" is not true when it comes to tenants. Some tenants miss their viewing by texting that they can't make it or last minute pulling out then lying. The worst moment for me is that unexpected text or call when tenant can't pay rent. Despite all the challenges, my favourite part was meeting different tenants and sharing their stories. Filling the rooms and noticing how happy the tenants are, finding deals and meeting like-minded people also give me a buzz.

Regardless of the problems, I knew, this was nothing compared to me going to work and not liking my job, wasting eight hours of my day then coming back home eating, watching TV and starting the cycle again. If the above challenges are going to make me more money than my job, give me more freedom and a lot less moaning, then it is all worth it.

I always remind myself of the value gained after a couple years learning regardless of the struggles. The outcome does not compare to working for someone else for the rest of my life. The challenges I have experienced helped me to develop a strong mindset, equip me with the skills to think outside the box and taught me resilience when facing rejections. Finally, not giving up and being consistent helped me to persevere and achieve my goal.

My experience in managing both rent-to-rent HMO's was tough at first, but no pain no gain. If you feel it is easy doing anything as an entrepreneur, you will fail. Life is about going through pain to gain success. After trial and error, I began to understand that building relationships with your tenants is key to success as they will help you. I have experienced several tenants' issues such as tenants losing their job or leaving prematurely due to unforeseen circumstances.

When you build a really good relationship the tenants can sometimes help you find new tenants to replace the ones that left. Other times, you just have to take it on the chin and learn from it. You will mentally suffer, I can guarantee this, you will have many sleepless nights, constant overthinking and possible emotional break downs, but, in the end, it will be all worth it.

If I survived fifteen years of my life working and not enjoying any of my jobs, I am sure you will be able to survive at least three years being a property entrepreneur. Learn from it, don't moan, be proactive and deal with it. No one owes you anything!

My advice to anyone starting their rent-to-rent business is; it is important to follow the process and work hard. If you have a weak mind or lazy, do not become a property investor. You have already failed before you start. Never feel as if you must do business on your own, talk to people, work with people and be honest about how you feel. Being an entrepreneur is lonely, but if you speak out you will find someone who is willing to listen to you and you can learn together. I have a good friend and we are planning to scale the business together.

Here are the top five tips I would love to leave you with:

1.   Read and learn about mindset.

2.   Follow the process.

3.   Know how to build relationships with agents, landlords and tenants from the start.

4.   Be flexible, understand how to resolve an issue if it arises.

5.   Be organised.

My goal is to become a mindset coach in the property business as I see too many people failing and I feel there is currently not enough in the industry. We should be enjoying the journey, not barely managing or coping. This is one of the reasons people fail, they do not know how to effectively manage their anxieties.

Go out there and do it. You've got this!

Duquarne Edwards

My journey in the property industry started back in 2016. I started out as a trainee lettings negotiator. My intentions in securing a job in an estate agency was to learn and understand the industry, then use the skills and knowledge I had gained to build a property business of my own. When and how would I do this? I was not certain. However, I knew that it would happen and when it did, I was going to do it big.

From a young age, I always had the desire of achieving the best in everything I did. This was repeatedly drilled into my head by my mum. Beside the encouragement I was given by my mum (who was a single mother raising two younger siblings). The environment I was raised in taught me many hard and life changing lessons, that would later prove to be the major influences in creating the spirit that would push me throughout my journey in business today.

I grew up in South London, an area which was heavily influenced by crime and gang culture. I was the product of a broken family which filled me with insecurities and a desperate search for my own identity.

My need to belong forced me into different unsavoury experiences such as, selling drugs, robberies and numerous street fights. At the age of fourteen, I was involved in a shooting that resulted in an imposed ban from my community.

By the time I was sixteen I had lost a few of my closest friends to gang violence. Although I was barred from my community, there were no major changes in my destructive lifestyle. I was still heavily involved in illegal activities.

There was no change on my horizon until I was involved in a street fight that almost cost my life. This was the trigger for me, I knew I had to take the initiative and find some sort of change.

Having experienced so much by the age of eighteen and still searching for a sense of self-identity I felt lost. I made the decision to begin a journey of self-discovery and found myself a mentor who helped me to change my perspective, the way I viewed myself and everything around me.

"Knowledge of self is the beginning of wisdom" he would say. I started to understand my own journey and draw the positives from everything I experienced in life, and the journey to a new future for myself began.

I learnt that hidden in every negative experience in life was a gift that should be embraced. Behind every obstacle or failure are lessons and tools needed to build you for the next stage towards the life we desire.

Looking back on my teenage experiences, I can clearly see that there were two-character traits that have proven very helpful in my journey thus far. The first was I always confronting my feelings of fear directly and the second was to go after what I wanted regardless of the cost. As with most people, the dream image you have of yourself is one where you have achieved great success in a particular field of endeavour, which is usually measured by status and wealth.

Growing up, I never had many examples of successful businessmen who started their own businesses to emulate. Most of my examples had followed the path to higher education and become a qualified professional in their field; a route that I knew from early, was not for me. I had little or no idea of how I would achieve the success I craved.

I had always been a forward thinker and I knew that unless I stepped out of my comfort zone, I would never accomplish my dreams. I was not prepared to be nothing more than an extra number in society as a permanent employee building another man's dream.

The desire for something different led me to start thinking outside the box. I was hungry for success. Every person I met who drove a nice car or had some form of tangible symbol of success, I wanted to know them. I spoke to and met many different people from traders to chain restaurant owners, business enthusiasts and successful professionals.

I asked questions and listened intently to their answers. There was one word that was consistent amongst all my conversation with them – property. They were involved with it directly or indirectly. Every successful person knew the importance of property.

It was strange to me because the only people I knew or imagined to be involved in property was either white or from the Asian community. I did not have a template for a black property entrepreneur. Despite this, I was determined to be successful and create my own template for future generations. The frequent repetition of this word amongst the people I aspired to be like meant I had to learn more about property!

My sojourn into a letting agent was the start of my property journey. I intended to learn from the bottom to the top. I was actively acting on what I instinctively believed. It was during my tenure at the estate agency that I met my joint venture and business partner Kingsley who has been on this journey with me ever since.

After a few conversations we both discovered that we saw life as well as property from a similar perspective and we both had the desire to pursue our own ventures in the future. As letting agents every month was a crazy scrabble to get deals and let properties. We were always looking for opportunities to let long term properties quickly and also successfully on a month by month basis.

Kingsley introduced me to Napa whom he had done business within the past. He explained that Napa was willing to rent properties from me on a regular basis as long as they suited his business model as a "Company Let".

I had heard this terminology used in previous business settings but had no in-depth knowledge or experience in this field. However, I did not let my lack of knowledge slow my ambition. If you do not know something you can always find out as long as you have the motivation to do so and I had the motivation. I took Napa on a few viewings and within a short space of time we built a professional relationship.

In one of our conversations, Napa explained to me that he made his money from properties that he did not own, by simply renting a property, offering a guaranteed fixed rent to the landlord and then re-renting the rooms to working professionals.

He told me in some cases he was able to make over £1000 a month from one deal. This was slightly less than my salary before commission, so I undoubtedly wanted to know more. Napa offered to mentor both Kingsley and I so we could gain a better understanding of the business and how to build a portfolio of our own.

We spent a few months learning new skills and gaining knowledge from Napa whilst fine tuning our skills as negotiators. After a few weeks we were finally ready to begin our journey in the world of rent-to-rent. The guidance offered by Napa taught us that if we were to make the transition from employees to becoming owners of our own rent-to-rent business, then we must understand the value of having a strong mindset. He explained the importance of believing on our product and the service we were offering to landlords if we were to succeed.

I took all the advice given by Napa and started a rent-to-rent business with my partner Kingsley. At present we have eleven properties, having secured our first two whilst still in employment. One of the highest cash flowing properties we have earns us a total £1300 and was secured by a referral from a fellow rent-to-rent investor. The investor did not pursue the deal as the location of the property was in an unfamiliar area.

The property was in the final stage of refurbishment, six bedrooms all with en-suites, a communal living area and garden. The landlord had a substantial mortgage and was very keen on getting a tenant as soon as possible. We managed to agree a thirty-day grace period with the landlord giving us access to the property thirty days before the beginning of our tenancy, without paying any rent or deposit. This gave us a chance to prepare the property for occupancy and secure tenants before our first rental payment was due.

Knowing that we needed furniture fast to attract tenants by taking suitable pictures of the house, we used a private investor to lend us some money on a short-term contract. The money was returned to them with interest at the end of the thirty-day period. Using rent paid in advance by tenants we were able to pay the landlords first month's rent and deposits, as well as the money back to our investor.

With only thirty days to fill the property and have enough money to pay the move in costs was a challenge. Coupled with that we also had to find suitable tenants. We advertised on portals such as Facebook, Gumtree, Zoopla (via letting agents) and Spare Room and we are able to source the majority of our tenants. With a few subtle adjustments to rental payments we were able to get all the rooms filled on time.

Life never runs smoothly for too long in business. A smart businessman knows how to prepare for these times. Shortly after all the tenants had moved in and just a few weeks of managing the property we discovered we had a troublesome tenant who had been causing tension amongst two other tenants within the house.

This is quite common in a communal living arrangement and most time the issue resolves itself without any external interference. This must always be monitored closely as it can potentially affect your business if matters escalate. Tenants may be left feeling uncomfortable, threatened or stressed and opt to vacate your premises. In rare scenarios they might even start speaking badly about the property and your management of the accommodations.

To diffuse the situation swiftly we intervened and after open and honest discussions, the tenant agreed that things were just not going to work, and we came to a mutual agreement to terminate her tenancy early to create peace within the household. It is better to lose one tenant rather than five. Despite the hiccups, it was extremely satisfying to know that we out-negotiated two other companies, secured the property with a substantial grace period and filled all rooms in time.

My first deal worked out well but not every deal secured turned out exactly as planned. There is a property in our portfolio located in Greenwich that was introduced to us by a rogue agent who later proved to be disingenuous and almost cost us the deal. We viewed the property and realised that only about half of the work had been completed to suit the HMO regulatory requirements. We were informed by the landlord that the rest would be finished before we took control of the property. It is a three-bedroom house with two reception rooms and two bathrooms.

We put forward an offer of the asking price as we knew the property would make us a minimum of £650 per month and it was quickly accepted. During the process we realised that we had not been referenced for the property after being offered a contract.

We decided to do our own research and noticed that the letting agent was not registered at Companies House and almost all the employees in the company were using aliases. When we tested the mode of communication that was offered, no one answered our telephone calls or replied to the emails we sent.

We had never experienced this before but naively we continued. We relied on the fact that the agent looked professional, spoke articulately and had keys to the house. What's the worst that could happen we reasoned?

After receiving the keys and signing the contract we started to arrange viewings for potential tenants. A few days later we noticed a sign on the window stating, "The landlord be will re-entering this property on Friday" and it was signed and dated by a solicitor. We became very nervous and very concerned. We went on a desperate search to find the landlord and find out what was going on.

We managed to arrange a meeting and discovered that the agent who actually introduced us to the property had been renting it for a number of years and had stopped paying rent. He had been using the property for illegal activities.

We were flabbergasted but it is when the going gets tough that the tough gets going. We were poised to lose thousands of pounds on this deal. Instead of writing this off as a major loss we decided to go after the deal with a passion. With some savvy negotiations and utilisation of skills learnt from being a letting agent we managed to salvage the deal. We were able to agree on a continuation of our arrangement without paying a deposit and instead using the money to finish the works for the HMO.

Unfortunately, fake agents have become a common scenario today, and it has definitely taught us to be more diligent in our research to find potential deals.

Presently we are still growing our portfolio but slowly and carefully. As we grow, we are turning our focus towards more advanced strategies of buying properties and we are working closely with investors to provide larger returns than the high street banks are able to offer within a shorter period of time!

Fontaine brothers

My name is Steven Fontaine and my brother/business partner is Dylan Fontaine. Together we are the Fontaine brothers.

We grew up with our mum and our youngest brother Liam. We didn't really have much financially, our clothes were from charity shops and our mum would often go without to make sure we have a meal. Our friends in school used to tell us things like how they got a TV for Christmas in their own bedroom. During these times, my mum didn't even have the money for a bed for me or herself because our dad left and took everything. Literally everything! Even down to the cutlery! We were left with nothing!

We may have lacked financially but we were never short of love and guidance from our mum.

I remember seeing her working in the freezing weathers, we had no car and if we were not in school, we would come along. I remember asking her why she works so many jobs when all of our neighbours claimed benefits. She explained to me that we all need money and we need to work hard for our money. She taught us so much with regards to strong work ethic and not being lazy. I do not remember a single time where she sat down and relaxed for 5 minutes throughout our childhood - I'm not even exaggerating!

I remember watching my mum work so hard just to make ends meet and I thought to myself, is this what we have to do? We're born, we go to school, we go to work, then we retire and die?

I told her that I didn't know what I wanted to do when I get older and she said: why don't you be a boss? I asked her what she meant, and she told me it's someone who gets people to work for them whilst they work on improving the business.

This sounded pretty good to me and my brother Dylan. We started walking around our school telling people 'I'm a boss'!

We were constantly thinking of ways to make money. I used to rake our garden for about an hour each weekend and got paid £1 each time. I remember I felt so happy when

122

I had saved £5 after five weeks. Shortly after, I was at a friend's house and he asked his mum for £5 to go out with and he got it, just like that... I remember thinking I need to upgrade my game and find a better way.

We started to find ways of making money in school.

We used to get £2 lunch money per day in school. Dylan used £1 of his lunch money to buy 5 packs of cheap biscuits in ASDA for his lunch for the week. By the end of the week he would have £9 saved. On the weekend he would buy 5 packs of biscuits for his lunch for the next week and with the money he saved, he would buy sweets and cans of drink that were on offer to sell in school to make a profit.

I used to ask people what DVDs they wanted to buy. I would charge them around £10 and order the DVD from eBay for around £2 or £3. I would take cigarettes from teachers and sell them in the playground.

I left school thinking all I need to do is get enough money, live poor and keep saving.

We then started getting ourselves in a lot of trouble and we were hanging around with the wrong people.

On the night of the 1st of December 2013, my house burnt down with my mum and my 13-year-old brother Liam inside. When I arrived at the scene, Liam had somehow rescued my unconscious mum from the fire and dragged her out of the house. The house and all its content, all our belongings, everything that we owned had gone up in flames.

Liam was getting in the ambulance with my mum who had hardly any skin left on her and he was the only passenger allowed to go with her so I told him I would meet him at the hospital. I asked one of the paramedics if my mum was going to die. She looked sad to tell me that its very likely as her lungs are closing.

I was scared and needed to be strong for my brother Liam, I literally had to show no fear, as I am his oldest brother (I was 18). We were now homeless, and I needed to make sure he had food, a place to stay and tried hard to cheer him up too. Luckily, we were already very mentally tough kids. He seemed pretty cool about things, he trusted me.

I felt I had no control; I didn't tell anyone what had happened because I was scared social services might separate us.

Long story short, my mum was in a coma for a while and was treated for her burns. She is alive and well now. The fire department awarded Liam for his bravery and told him if it wasn't for his actions that night, we would be orphans. He is a hero and we are so lucky our mum is still here with us.

It was a huge wake up call for me and my brother Dylan. We knew we needed to stop hanging around with the wrong crowd and we never wanted to be in a position where we feel we don't have enough money to help in a serious situation.

I got a job in a factory and was giving 100 percent effort at all times so I could reach the best paid target. I was working the night shift because it was an extra £1 per hour and I was doing overtime 7 days a week. I saw this job as a place to save enough money to start some kind of business. I didn't know what the business was going to be. I knew I wanted to be a businessman.

I met someone in the factory called Michael Seatory. He was also very interested in business. He told me about making money work for me rather than working for money. Michael completely changed my mindset on life, money, business and so many of my personal battles. We soon realised our pasts were quite similar and we also had a massive fire in our belly and desire for more in life. He told me about Robert Kiyosaki's books, and we would talk every single night shift about business.

We eventually partnered up and starting building companies. One company was buying Segway hoverboards from China when they first came out and selling them around the UK. Another company was in affiliate marketing. Another one was buying and selling brand-able domain names and more.

We went through so many failures, mistakes and had a lot of success too. We made some money and we lost some too. We didn't have any mentor or anyone to help us. We just started and never stopped. We continued working our jobs and any money we got was reinvested. During these times I learnt so much about business and experienced so many highs and lows. It's not for the feint hearted, it's tough and it's not an easy ride!

Dylan was doing really well in a sales job at the time and was religiously watching Grant Cardone videos. He was consistently the top performer. He was constantly trying to improve in sales, even buying Grant Cardone's training programs. He understood the importance of investing in himself to improve. He got me a job there and this is where I learnt how to sell, get a thick skin and overcome rejection. Dylan spoke to me about setting up a sales company, this sounded like a great idea but there was a minor issue - we had no money!

I went to the bank and asked for an overdraft and they gave me £2,000. I was shocked and called Dylan and told him to do the same. He did and it worked! We now had £4,000 and thought to ourselves let's quit our jobs, buy what we need to start and live off the rest.

We bought a printer, phone systems and bought a list of people from a data collection company and started phoning this list trying to sell our product. In these times we learnt so much about taking massive action because we literally had to. We were doing 700 calls each every day. If we didn't sell our product the bills wouldn't be paid, and we wouldn't survive.

Once we got the ball rolling, we decided not to pay ourselves and continued to live off the rest of our overdraft. This meant we could employ people quicker. A couple months later we had 5 people calling customers in our living room and we began to grow. Even when our company was growing, we decided not to pay ourselves. Instead we continued to live off our overdraft as cheap as possible literally scraping by each month. We were still only really eating pot noodles and bread so we could save extra to invest more.

We started to look at large companies, companies that always seem to be there. What are they doing right? We discovered that huge insurance companies and very wealthy people tend to invest heavily in real estate, and it was always something Dylan and I were very interested in.

The reason we chose the rent-to-rent HMO model was because it meant we could generate cash flow with little money to put down. We also saw rent-to-rent as a 'try before you buy'. Our plan was to gain experience and expert knowledge before we eventually start purchasing property.

Straight away we decided to watch hours and hours of YouTube videos trying to understand the strategy. We read books and attended property events. We eventually felt we knew everything we needed to know to get started. We tried and tried to get a deal but there were always one or two things we got stuck on or didn't understand every time we got close.

My brother Dylan read Napa's book "The Rent-to-Rent Blueprint" and spoke to me about his mentorship. Dylan was definitely up for it. However, we both were sceptical. Eventually we spoke with Napa on the phone and we realised straight away he was a very genuine person; he did not avoid any questions. He was just very honest, so we went for it.

Napa told us how to set up the company, get compliant and decide on a target area. He told us to do it straight away and he'll call us the following week. We did that.

He then told us to start recording ourselves calling agents outside of our target area for practice. We then sent him the call recordings for him to review and tell us how to improve.

The following week we started calling in our targeted area. At this point we decided to vlog everything we were doing and thought if it goes well or if it goes wrong, we will upload it on our YouTube Channel 'Fontaine Brothers'. We wanted to show the good, the bad and the ugly because no one was really sharing their failures or their full journey on YouTube.

We had many agents telling us they were not interested in what we do, and we had the phone put down on us plenty of times.

We sent out lots of direct to vendor letters. Still filming the whole process for YouTube, Dylan eventually arranged a block viewing with an agent who wanted to show us a few properties.

Finally, some success!

When we got to the letting agents, they told us that the girl we spoke to was new and they do not want to work with us.

We started hammering the phones again and got another agent to say yes. We went to view more properties with another agent, but the deals didn't stack up at all.

We were getting stressed because it felt like we wasted the whole week. We sat in the car and started to call more agents, after a few calls, we got another yes.

We went to view the properties. They were good deals and we knew we could make a good offer on them, so we got home, did our due diligence and emailed an offer across.

Within 8 days of calling agents, doing viewings and making offers we had 2 offers accepted.

Once we had the offers accepted, the letting agents forwarded the contracts for us to sign. We knew nothing about contracts, so we called Napa. He connected us with a great guy who helped us negotiate better terms as there were a few things that needed amending.

I signed and we went to grab the keys!

We secured an 8-bed property and a 7-bed property. The properties are right next door to each other which makes it easier for conducting viewings to potential tenants.

The 8 bed has 2 bathrooms and a toilet room. The 7 bed has a shower room and a bathroom. They both already had HMO licences in place.

The total rent for both deals is £3800, and we can rent out each room for an average of £475. We pay the bills and cover minor maintenance issues. Altogether we are left with between £2,200 - £2,500 profit each month when fully occupied.

The day we got the keys to the property we started clearing all the rubbish, got rid of all the old furniture and ordered the new furniture from IKEA.

We got some paint and got cracking straight away whilst vlogging everything for our YouTube channel.

The properties needed a light refurb.

Halfway through completing the first property, Dylan's car broke down and we had already spent almost all of our savings that we had at that time. We wanted to make sure we had enough money to pay the landlord before getting a car. We had to sleep on the sofas in the properties as they are an hour drive from where we live, and we done that until the properties were completely ready for tenants.

Our plan was to use the tenant's money once they move in to buy a car and get home after we've paid the landlord.

Altogether it cost around £5,000 to get both of the properties to the right standard for our prospective tenants. We used this money to buy paint, beds, wardrobes, bed side tables, lamps, sofas, tables, chairs and much more.

All the furniture needed replacing in both properties. We underestimated how long it would take both of us to get the properties ready. It took so long that we ended up having to pay the first month's rent - with no tenants. This meant the total entry cost was around £9,000.

At first, we only cared about getting tenants to move in. We had not really taken much time to actually think of all the tenants as a collective. Would they argue? Would they cause problems with each other? Is it better to stick to a certain age group? We just got any tenants in fast.

We are currently tenanting the second property as I write this. In this property we will take more time to think of the tenants as a collective rather than each individual tenant. We have been given advice by some great people who are very good at creating a nice community within their HMO properties so that the tenants prefer to stay longer.

We source most of our tenants through spare room and Facebook marketplace. We have also established relationships within our area with people doing a similar thing. We often get referred tenants through connections we have made with landlords who are getting enquiries but are fully tenanted.

We aim for tenants aged between 25-40. We make sure that they are working and do reference checks on all tenants that want to move in. When taking the prospective tenants on viewings, we ask as many questions as possible so that we can make a final decision based on our gut feeling.

So far, we have had no issues with tenants; it has actually been simpler than we had originally thought. We know that eventually we will get issues but it's all part of the experience. We are also willing to manage anyone's HMO or property (that fits our criteria) in the Dorset/Hampshire areas. If you are a deal sourcer and have HMO or single let properties in those areas, we can manage them for your investors. Likewise, if you are an investor or a landlord, we would be happy to help. You can inquire on this email: info@fontainemanagement.co.uk

The next deals we take we will:

- Take more time to plan out the work

- Find as many people as possible who are willing to help

- Work out a realistic deadline for work required to be completed.

The part we enjoyed most about managing tenants is the new learning experience. The next challenge will be training and managing staff to do the management.

The only thing we dislike about managing property is knowing that we could have someone do this for us whilst we get more deals. Right now, we need to generate more cash flow and make that possible.

If I'm honest, getting the deal was quite easy. This is mainly down to having a mentor and a very strong desire. There were so many things we came across that we just couldn't understand. We would call Napa each time we hit a brick wall and by the end of the call we would know what to do next.

The hardest part was agreeing on the contracts. It took around a month. It was a stressful time, but it worked out in the end because we had the right connections thanks to Napa.

Our main struggle in the beginning was being patient. We were relentlessly trying to get a deal and each day that went past was seriously stressing us out.

We got around this by putting in massive action. If we put the work in, we know eventually it's going to happen for us, and we had no doubt we would get there. We have learnt to love the stress and the stress slowly is becoming excitement.

Mentorship has helped us massively. A lot of people believe that mentorship is a waste of money and anyone can do it all on their own. Although this may be true in some cases, we may have been able to do it without Napa, but it would have cost us so much more money, a huge amount of time and we probably would not have set up the legalities correctly. For us it was a game changer, if we ever get into a different strategy, we would always make sure we have a mentor. For us it is essential.

It's good to have someone to hold you accountable but for us, we are good at keeping ourselves accountable. We really benefited from being able to call Napa in any situation or problem we faced, and he would help us and give us advice based on his past experiences. The value we got out of it was priceless plus he has saved us thousands of pounds on the refurb of the property just by coming over when we got the keys.

The best moment for us is the whole learning experience. We love to learn new ways of making money, improving our situation and fighting for the best results when under pressure. Most of all we just love making deals. The bigger the better, big scary out of comfort zone types of deals! Also, meeting people who are like minded. The property game has introduced us to some really incredible people.

The worst part is feeling like you're not going anywhere. That's the worst possible feeling. It has not been easy but the only thing that would have stopped us is death and we will to continue to grow!

It's going to sound like Napa is paying me to say this but getting the right mentor was the best thing we could have done. I mean that and I am forever grateful for the help, patience, knowledge and instant support he has given us.

Napa's mentoring was huge. We may have been able to do it without him as I mentioned earlier but why would we waste our money and time on making mistakes and getting things wrong when for an affordable amount of money, we can leverage his 4-5 years of experience and fast track our success?

No brainer.

We have learnt so much in this journey and as I am writing this it has only been around 3 months since we started.

Here is our top 5 take away:

- Understanding the pitfalls in all business models

- Start now because it will never be the right time to start so just start right now and learn on the job

- Be yourself. If you try to act like someone you're not or tell lies you will soon be caught out. You would be surprised how many people actually like you for just being yourself.

- Get a good network of people that can help you! Network like crazy. Every day on all social media.

- Make sure what you're doing is 100% legal & ethical.

Follow our journey on YouTube - Fontaine Brothers

Jake Aldric

Rent-to-rent appealed to me as it is a low money down strategy, and I decided I would commit to this strategy. I first did a 1-2-1, one day rent-to-rent course with Napa before I joined his three months gold mentoring program.

The mentoring was very valuable. I learned a lot from Napa as he guided me step by step on how to set up my business with compliance and then gave me advice on how to find deals. I didn't have any savings to invest in my own deals, so he showed me ways I could position myself on social media to attract joint venture partners. This was one of the most valuable things I've learned.

My target area is Article 4, so we decided to focus on properties with an HMO license. There are multiple universities in my target area, so we targeted empty student properties on Rightmove and booked days of block viewings. To practice calling agents, Napa told me to find

140

another city with Article 4 and practise calling the agents there. After doing quite well booking viewings in the other areas, I got started in my area.

Napa came with me to the first day of viewings, I think we put in a total of ten offers from eleven viewings and all were rejected. I worked full time, so I would spend my lunch break booking viewings for my time off. I was putting in offers regularly, and they were all rejected regularly. After nearly three months, I finally had some offers accepted. I managed to find a joint venture (JV) partner but the deal fell through at the contracts stage as we couldn't agree on the terms.

After this deal, I met an investor who said although these deals didn't work, he would be interested in joint venturing with me. Before committing myself to this investor I also spoke with a number of people that seemed really interested to invest. However, when I brought the deal to the table all the investors had vanished.

Napa gave me some great advice about general property investing and finding deals, so I got back into the game with a plan. I would book viewings in the day and attend networking events in the evenings.

The first two viewings were with an agent I had worked with previously, so I knew the agent was on board with what we were doing. That afternoon, I submitted my offers and then went to my first networking event. I told the people on my table what I was doing and there was an agent who said he had a rent-to-rent deal available in my area.

He asked me to call him in the morning so we could arrange a viewing. The first thing next morning, I contacted the agent from the networking event and arranged to see the property next day. The property was good with new carpets and recently painted. It was in a good area and the numbers looked reasonable, so I secured the deal with the agent. One of my offers from the previous day also got accepted.

Napa helped at every stage, from setting up the business, setting daily tasks, advice on sourcing deals, attending a day of viewings, advice on joint ventures and WhatsApp support when needed throughout the process.

My first five months managing the properties was not plain sailing. I made a few mistakes early which caused delays in renting the rooms.

I have had tenant issues, maintenance issues and a non-paying tenant. Thankfully I have a good network of experienced colleagues, so I often ask for advice on what to do when a problem arises. Managing a property business while working full time has not been easy. My advice to anybody starting rent-to-rent with no property/HMO management experience is:

- Work hard and keep a positive attitude.
- Take every situation as it comes as it is inevitable there will be problems and obstacles.
- Ask for advice when problems arise.
- A good mindset is also vital.

Kenan Buckley

My name is Kenan Buckley and I am twenty-five years old. I am a self-employed gas engineer and plumber who lives in Birmingham.

I initially discovered the rent-to-rent strategy when I visited a property seminar in London after seeing a Facebook ad in December 2018. The seminar sounded too good to be true, so I decided to research on YouTube, read books and join a property academy.

Whilst I was self-educating on rent-to-rent and property, I was working full time with the aim of securing a mortgage. However, in the month of April, I decided to change my goal when it dawned on me that my ten thousand pounds investment for the purpose of a deposit, furniture, white goods would become a liability. In addition, the property was not below market value (BMV) and it would have taken me a long time to save another ten thousand pounds. So, I thought about it and asked myself, what if I could turn that £10K into £20K?

That is when I took a big leap of faith.

After reading about the rent-to-rent strategy, I wasn't filled with absolute confidence in analysing deals. Plus, I had a few gaps in my knowledge. I decided to join Napa's mentorship in May 2019 to get the ball rolling.

The mentoring helped me in many ways with self-confidence, knowledge, understanding how to position myself, how to deal with agents in real life and more. I needed the extra guidance for reassurance as I am sure you would agree that it is better to learn from others' mistakes rather than make them yourself. Therefore, I learnt from an experienced mentor in the desired field!

I found my first rent-to-rent deal in June 2019 on Rightmove. I contacted the agent to ask if they accepted company lets. Once they confirmed that they accepted company lets, a viewing was booked on a four-bedroom HMO. A week later I secured my first HMO.

Unfortunately, due to hidden infestation and my own fears and mistrust of the agent, I decided to hand back the keys. I lost money on this deal but in hindsight it was a blessing. I did learn a lot about agents, how to be more thorough and how to control my emotions.

Some self-employed people struggled to pass the referencing stage, and this was a major obstacle. However, if you are creative you can overcome it. I passed my referencing as a self-employed person easily. Firstly, I needed to prove I had a stable income so I made sure I earned enough money consistently (£1.8K) to prove to an agent I could take on that responsibility.

In addition, I had some savings in my account; please bear in mind, my first rent-to-rent rent was £850 per month. I was not looking for rents in excess of £1000 because I like to take calculated risks and be confident that if things are not going according to plan then I still have a chance of surviving.

My strategy is rent low instead of rent high, but this will differ depending on your attitude to risk. I know that if my deals are not working then I can afford to plug the gaps with cash from my side jobs. I would advise you to do the same. Do not chase after every shiny penny and carefully calculate your risks.

I must admit throughout my first rent-to-rent ordeal I was indecisive about what to do and my mind kept switching between rent-to-rent HMO or rent-to-rent serviced accommodations (SA). I then chose to move forward with my mind firmly fixed on SA, but I would look for areas where my properties would work as a SA and an HMO as an exit strategy.

After returning my first rent-to-rent deal to the agent, I came across another deal a month later from a letting company I visited two and a half months prior whilst on the hunt for HMO's. It is a good idea to keep a record of who you spoke to, when and where, just in case you cross paths again. I was so determined to make my plan work I visited all the letting managers in my gold mine area so they could remember me the next time I called.

In July 2019 I secured a property on a two-year lease and invested five thousand pounds of my own money as no one wanted to invest in me at that time due to a lack of funds and their belief in me. I thought the only way I could get others to trust me is by trusting in myself and putting my money where my mouth was. By creating my own luck, I managed to accommodate an Irish building firm on a six-month lease which is generating thirteen hundred pounds in profit and they are looking to extend by another month due to the current coronavirus crisis.

My main aim in using these niche property strategies is to generate enough income to supplement my self-employed life so I decided to secure another SA in December 2019, which is currently accommodating a company from Austria and they are working at Land Rover in Birmingham. Profit from this current deal is £1.5K for thirty-five nights.

To secure this deal, my friend loaned me twelve hundred pounds, after witnessing my success on the first rent-to-rent SA. I ensured I documented the whole process via Facebook, as showcasing your successes can benefit your business in the future.

I was very happy that someone trusted in my plan and vision. I agreed to return his money within eight months, but the property started off so well I generated enough profit to return his loan in just two months. It was a great feeling. I am currently in the process of recouping my initial investment back on this property as I believe we must pay off our debts first and then begin to reap the rewards after.

I manage both of my properties because I have systemised the business, so it does not require much effort from me. Initially it was a nightmare as I did not have much knowledge or experience. I learnt what I could, trusted in my abilities of finding a good deal and I did. I am currently in talks about getting one of my properties on a lease option.

Please bear in mind, as quick as the process may seem, it took many phone calls, late nights learning and sacrifices. My best advice to those who wish to embark on their rent-to-rent journey is to first establish your WHY. Before you invest in a strategy you need to understand it and surround yourself with the right people who are on the same path as you.

I have been vlogging my whole journey since March 2019, if you wish to connect, be motivated or inspired then subscribe to my YouTube channel Kenan Buckley and add me on Facebook.

These are my five top tips that I would like to share with you:

1.Take time to understand the strategy.

2. Do not always believe in everything you see in property. Question everything. Remember it is your neck and money on the line.

3. Do not chase after shiny pennies.

4. Triple check your numbers.

5. If you pick a mentor, make sure he is deeply involved with a property strategy, in other words, he lives and breathes it.

Richard Greaves

I grew up in an ordinary house without a father because he abandoned his son before he was born. I had love from my immediate and extended family to compensate for the absence of my dad. I was the white sheep of the family and everyone always showed me love. I was called Richie by my mum. I always felt as if I was not meant to be here today. Twenty-five years ago, before I came on to this earth my mother fought for me. She had a choice to choose me or herself to be saved from a pregnancy that was meant to go wrong. The strong woman that she is, decided to choose me. My family prayers and fights kept both me and her alive. I grew up with identity issues, not knowing what I wanted or who I wanted to be.

I did not go to university, but I did an apprenticeship for a bandwidth company which was generating two hundred and fifty million pounds in revenue each year. I was head hunted by the CEO through a dragon's den panel. I

151

was never a technical guy, I enjoyed interacting with people and learning much more than the actual job. I had the opportunity to surf around different departments in order to understand the fundamentals of the business. I had no plans or thoughts about leaving my job at this time.

I was then hit by the death of a close friend. It was my first experience seeing someone that was like a brother die. This happened two months before his wedding day. I was meant to be his groomsman. The sudden loss had a major impact on me. I struggled to make sense of everything.

A month before he passed away, I was homeless and slept on buses and in restaurants. This was a very hard period for me. It was made harder because my friend who passed away had helped me to find my identity. He had helped me to realise there was more inside of me than I ever knew. He believed in me more than I believed in myself.

We all go through these periods in our lives where we must look in the mirror and ask ourselves, do we want to continue following someone else's path or create our own? After my friend's death I had a lot of time alone and this was the best time of my life, not because of the experience I went through but because of what the experience created. It created an individual who recognised that life and death are not too far from each other and we must make decisions every day that could alter our path.

I decided I wanted to take control of my life and leave a legacy of myself for generations to come. For many years I went to seminars and meetings to better myself and understand the true value of money, how to manage and generate it. I always had the knowledge through YouTube videos, books, mentors and friends. My problem was, I had the knowledge but no results. I was that guy in the seminar that would be pumped up after the property session was done and ready to sign up. However, I never had any funds to cover a course. Then I would say I don't have it and go home with even more knowledge but still zero results.

I started thinking to myself, "you're surviving but when are you going to start living Rich?" I got together with some friends and told them I wanted to get into the property business. I just didn't know where or when and most importantly how? One of my friends then mentioned he went to school with Napa Bafikele and that he is mentoring people who want to make money in property, especially through rent-to-rent. I had heard about rent-to-rent before at the seminars I attended but never understood how it worked.

The initial meeting with Napa happened and I left believing that this can really happen. He didn't try to sell to me or make me feel as if I had to sign up. I was impressed. I saw that he was transparent. He told me there would be hard times, and it was not an easy process. Once again, I was ready, but there was only one problem, I didn't have enough money to sign up. Then I had to decide, do I want to build someone's else's legacy or create my own legacy for generations to come?

I took everything I had at the time, I didn't pay my rent and some bills in order to get enough money to sign up to Napa's mentorship programme. This is a risk many people would not take, but not many have been in my shoes where you have been homeless or had days when you didn't have food to eat. Days when you would have to take sugar from stores to eat or searching to find free handouts or use apps such as Olio to find where people give away food. I did not want that life anymore; I didn't want to go there again.

I started my training with an intensive first day where I learnt the fundamentals such as being compliant, what I wanted for my business, marketing, dealing sourcing et cetera. I started as soon I had the documents and became complaint. Whatever I needed Napa was there to help and give guidance.

I needed a guarantor and an investor due to my lack of finance and large portfolio contacts. Napa helped with an investor who had over fifty thousand pounds that she wanted to be invested. I was pumped up and ready. I found my first deal one month later. It was two properties with the same agency. These two properties generated seventeen hundred pounds per month in profit. I found this deal on Gumtree. I went to view both four-bedroom properties. They were ten minutes' drive away from each other, in a prime location. We started the referencing process and it all went wrong. I lost my first deal.

Two months later I managed to secure another deal I had found on Rightmove. It was a six-bedroom HMO. The house was massive with three floors and a garden with a car space. It had two bathrooms and one ensuite on the top floor. The rental price was £3540 per month but I negotiated down to £3350 per calendar month. I did not have a guarantor, and this is a big deal for most agencies. I offered a solution of two months' rent in advance and the five-week deposit which made the upfront cost £10,800. The agents also charged me a £900 fee which brought the total to £11,700.

This deal was a struggle because mentally I had so many deals that went wrong, but I had to believe this was my legacy that I was creating for myself. I had to meet the landlord face to face in the property. Napa also came along because this was my first deal and I did not want to take any chances and lose the deal. At the end of the meeting the landlord was happy, and we agreed with the next steps to take on this property. The only issue was… Where would I get the £11,700 from?

I know people do not just give out nearly £12K unless you have a proven track record, or they truly believe you have got a good deal when the numbers stacked up. I had a couple of days to get a potential investor onboard. Many people were interested but a few did not believe I would make £900 profit every month. One day before deadline to make payment and I still did not have any investor. I told Napa that I had two potential investors who were checking the numbers and the details, but it was cutting it too close for comfort.

To my surprise. my mentor showed his faith in me and became my investor. Napa took the deal and invested in this deal. Everything proceeded and we got the keys to the property. The next hurdle was to get the house ready to go on the market for professionals.

I painted the house and added new furniture. It had a deep clean with new bed sheets and pillows. I staged the beds myself and got a professional photographer to take pictures to put it onto the market. We first advertised on Spare Room, Facebook, Shpock, and Gumtree. The best results came from Spare room. It was hard to get tenants because it was my first time. Finding the right tenants is very important. I did my research through the internet and collected references.

The house was eventually filled, and my next challenge was managing the house. Since I had experience managing a team of thirty people on a weekly basis, I was ready for this challenge. Screening for good tenants is very important because they will help you by fixing or sorting little things, they can do rather than bothering you in the middle of the night. Over time I figured out how to fix most maintenance issues with help from, Napa, YouTube and friends.

This deal is currently generating £1,100 pcm. £200 more than I had predicted. Those investors who did not believe in me might be upset now as they missed a great opportunity. Hopefully they will invest in future projects as I slowly build my credibility in the market. I have now paid Napa back the entire £11,700 within 7 months. Now we are making money each month as joint venture partners.

My question to you is, do you choose to build the legacy of your employer? Or will you choose to build your own?

Attila Rizo

I've been following Attila's journey on social media and I was very impressed with the level of resilience he demonstrated. One of my mentoring packages allows a client to request me spending some time at their gold mine area.

My mentee was based in Manchester and requested me to go assist him with a meeting he had with a landlord. I shared on my Facebook that I was going Manchester and Attila messaged me privately if we could meet after the meeting. We met briefly and he had some questions he wanted to ask me. I felt his determination on how he really wanted to make this journey a success.

Just to clarify that I never trained or mentored Attila but I am heavily attracted to what he has done and achieved so far; I strongly believe his story would help many people in similar situation.

Here is Attila's story:

First of all, I would like to thank Napa for giving me the opportunity to share my story in this book.

My name is Attila Rizo, a Hungarian guy born in Romania, now living in Manchester.

I grew up living with my mum in the east side of Hungary, I had quite a normal life as a child and faced many challenges as I did not enjoy any school curriculum especially the English Language. At the age of 16 I could not speak English as I had no interest in learning it, however, my motive changed due to my interest in movies, I was fed up watching movies with subtitles. Therefore, I made a conscious decision to learn English and hired a private tutor.

I dedicated everything I had to get better with my English, within a few years my effort paid off, I was able to read and speak English fluently. I then went onto University to study English, American Literature and History.

I've always been eager to live abroad in places like the UK, but I lacked courage to follow my ambition. While I was at University in 2009 my mum purchased a property for me to live in during my study years. The property boasted with extra rooms that I rented to my friends. This allowed me to have some company and benefit from additional income generated from rent my friends were paying.

I'm a Manchester United fan and my affinity for the club keeps on getting stronger as time moves along. In December 2012 I decided to attend a game at Old Trafford for the very first time. I had a tremendous experience and based upon that I started to contemplate migrating to Manchester.

In 2014 a childhood friend from Hungary who lived in Manchester was looking for someone to buddy up with in order to rent a property. He presented the opportunity to me and I grabbed it with both hands instantly. I once read "if a window of opportunity appears, don't pull down the shade". Taking time to think whether I should move to Manchester was ludicrous, I immediately purchased a flight ticket to the next plane to Manchester. One of my best friends was also attracted to the idea so he packed his bag and joined me to the move in Manchester.

Thinking of it now moving to Manchester was very risky and challenging as I had no money, no national insurance number therefore I could not work. The living condition was atrocious I shared room with two of my friends for months.

I finally managed to sort out my paperwork and secured a job at a warehouse working nightshift. This was a turning point in my life as I was having some income coming in, though I did not enjoy the job, but I was grateful for having one.

Financially I became stable and moved out from the room I was sharing with two of my friends. I became a Manchester United season ticket holder and attending games was a dream. In addition, it was actually the main reason I migrated to Manchester. At this point life was great, everything was sailing smooth and I became comfortable, I lost drive, desire and ambition. I devoted my spare time going to Manchester United games and getting drunk every weekend. I literally did nothing that was constructive to better my life, I had no goals, no purpose and living life without direction.

I was quite of a big drinker and would be drinking 8 cans of beers before every football game. I no longer wanted to live this lifestyle as it was not fulfilling and deteriorating my health. Just like I made a conscious decision to learn English at my teen years, I made that same conscious decision never to drink anything but water. This decision refocused me, I started to read books and educate myself.

My mindset towards life, money and time totally changed when I read Rich Dad, Poor Dad by Robert Kiyosaki. I noticed that exchanging my time for money will never help me achieve my goals.

I started to research various avenues I could make investments where money would be working for me, rather than me exchanging my time for it. Property has always been on my mind since I've experienced passive income from the property my mum purchased for me to live in while I was at University. I still receive rental income from that property as I rented it out since I now live in the UK.

One of the obstacles I had was the belief that investing in property requires large sum of capital to commence. As I did not have large pot of savings it was a turn off for me. Throughout my research I came across various property strategies that did not require large capital to invest.

I was enticed with rent-to-rent due to the fact that you can control someone's asset and make a profit from it. I wanted to learn more about rent-to-rent, therefore, I watched countless hours of YouTube contents, I attended events, I read Napa's first book The Rent-to-Rent Blueprint alongside with other property books.

I gathered enough information and acknowledged that rent-to-rent was the strategy that I wanted to accomplish.

John Crosby once said, "mentoring is a brain to pick, an ear to listen, and a push in the right direction". I did not want to embark on this journey without a mentor, I wanted someone that can guide me, show me the correct way of building my business, someone I can report back to when I am facing challenges, and I found just that in January 2019.

I was very excited and motivated to get the ball rolling, my main strategy to secure rent-to-rent deals was to go via agents. I was so determined that I failed to select one area to devote my energy to. I relentlessly contacted agents in numerous areas and some were very far from where I lived, as I do not drive it made the task difficult. This is something I would not recommend anyone to do, what I have learned now is to focus one area you can commute to with ease.

In Liverpool agents were more receptive with the concept of rent-to-rent and I managed to secure my first deal, a 4-bedroom house. The property needed a light refurbishment I was eager to do since it was my first property and I wanted to do everything right. One of the major issues was finding tenants and I came into realisation that the property was not in a suitable location.

After hard work and dedication, I tenanted all four rooms, however, the profit generated was significantly lower than expected and the effort required was not worth keeping the deal. After intense consideration and thoughts, I came into conclusion that it would be better to exercise my clause of terminating the agreement early.

Learning from my past errors I now decided to source properties where I reside and areas in close proximity. Little did I know the areas I chose letting agents were not interested letting to any rent-to-rent operator. I came across a great deal of rejections from agents and landlords. This was emotionally challenging as I felt like my journey was staggered, I experience different types of negative emotions as I felt my goals were getting further and further away. At one point I had 40 rejections in a row which was pretty disheartening.

I started to question myself whether I am destined to achieve any level of success doing rent-to-rent, I questioned my ability, skills and knowledge. Then I remembered that the hardest battles are given to the strongest soldier. I took couple of days off then I started calling agents again. As Oprah Winfrey said, "I don't want anyone who doesn't want me", my mindset was that I only need to find one agent who believes in me and the strategy than I will blossom.

Finally, I called an agent that had in-depth knowledge about rent-to-rent and was very determined to work with me as he understood the benefit. The agency had a 6 bedroom already licensed HMO property, I arranged to view the property, after doing my due diligence I submitted my offer. I was excited when I received an email stating that the offer was accepted. The property needed a light refurbishment and I hired an interior designer to work with me on this project. I sent the agency and landlord the pre and post refurbishment pictures of the property. The landlord was very impressed with my performance and pledged to give me more properties in the future.

When the property was fully tenanted, I decided to start contacting agents again for more potential deals, while waiting for my current landlord to bring me more properties, I had miniature prosperity with other agents. Therefore, I decided to cultivate the relationship with my current agent whom I got the deal from.

During the lockdown in early 2020 the agent emailed me with a brand new 6-bedroom HMO asking if I was interested to take on a long let. After conducting my due diligence and I was excited to add another property onto my portfolio. Both properties are estimated to cash flow £800 each when is fully tenanted. The first property is already fully tenanted, and the second property only has one vacant room to be tenanted.

I just want to clarify that rent-to-rent is not an easy strategy as Napa always says that it's a business that need to be treated like one. My journey has been full of challenges including rejections, self-doubting and uncertainty. Prior having my breakthrough with an agent that understood rent-to-rent and was willing to work with me, the hardest part of my journey was finding such agency that comprehend the strategy.

I have yet to find any challenges managing both HMOs, I am aware that soon or later I will experience the usual property challenges such as difficult tenants, miss rental payments or voids periods. But to be brutally honest this is way better than having a boss as I feel I am doing something constructive and it's a step towards my goals. Most importantly I am in control of my time.

My tips to anyone that wants to get involved with rent-to-rent are:

1. Find at least 3-4 areas where you can do rent-to-rent and make sure it's not far from you.

2. Once you've taken a property and carried out some refurbishment work, make sure you send the pre and post refurb pictures to the agent and landlord.

3. Don't just focus on one strategy of finding rent-to-rent deals, make sure you have various approach too.

4. You can be direct with agents by asking straight if their work with rent-to-rent operators, chances are they already know what rent-to-rent is and you do not have to explain the benefit to them.

5. If you begin to feel like giving up and start doubting yourself due to the hardship on your journey, remind yourself why you have started.

I hope my journey can enlighten you to be resilient and consistent. Your WHY will keep you going when times get difficult.

I am looking to expand my rent-to-rent portfolio and I'm open to work with investor. If you are interested to work with me, please do not hesitate to contact me on social media.

Good luck!

It would be dishonest of me to just share success stories of mentees I have worked with. I've worked with numerous mentees that did not managed to secure any rent-to-rent deal, in fact in 2019 I mentored 30 students and 14 mentees secured rent-to-rent deals whereas the rest did not. This does not mean they are failures, remember, as I mentioned earlier rent-to-rent is not an easy strategy to embark upon, even with the help of a mentor.

I have yet to witness any trainer, mentor, coach or educational system that produce 100% success rate.

I've asked few mentees to share their stories and experiences on rent-to-rent even though no deal was secured, I believe there's a lesson to be learned.

Trisha Nzau

My name is Trisha Nzau and I am a mindset coach, author & public speaker. Before I became a mindset coach. I was mentored by Napa. I came across Napa on social media and realised he was quite local and very experienced, so it made sense for me to be mentored by him.

Prior to this property venture I had no intentions on getting into property but as I was a first-time mum on maternity leave. Every morning I would religiously watch homes under the hammer which then caught my attention to invest a bit more time on how this property world works.

I used to think I need to be at least rich to invest in property and the more I researched the more it became apparent to me that there are a number of strategies to get my foot on the property ladder without needing to invest much money.

I went to a few free training courses which were just teaching what I had already known, and it would end with up selling a course, but I didn't feel it was genuine, it felt more like they just wanted my money. However, it was a great experience as I met like-minded people.

At this point I decided to go for the rent-to-rent strategy as the entry cost was low in comparison to other property strategy. The return of investment was good enough that after 4 properties I can potentially be financially free. This hungered my spirit to get deals quickly.

So, I eventually found a coach, but he lived quite far away. So, I came across Napa and was watching him for a while to see if he was trustworthy. I did do research on him through other people's feedback and my gut instinct just told me to go for him.

Initially I picked up bad habits, up until the point I met Napa, I self-taught myself and he had to basically recondition my knowledge and structure a plan. At this time, I was quite enthusiastic and filled with adrenaline so getting the work done was the quite easy.

As silly as it may sound, I know the role of a mentor, but I think I expected more. Which was wrong. A mentor's job is to give the information you need for your business and support whenever necessary under the terms and conditions. Subconsciously it's easy to blame your mentor when things don't go your way. All mentors do is give you information and it's up to you what you do with it. It's so important to also do your own due diligence.

I started feeling like everyone was getting deals and I wasn't then I started doubted whether this was for me or not. To be honest I was driven by the thought of the potential capital I can raise through this strategy. Being a first-time mum, everything is still new so it's hard to run a business and readjust life. I didn't consider how my circumstance may affect my mobility to visit agent or view properties.

In actual fact I didn't set up a system which will enable me to manage my business as well as personal life, so everything took a toll on me. I disconnected from social media as I felt it became overwhelming with other people success stories. Over time I knew I was dragging my feet in this strategy because my heart wasn't in it so mentally, I clocked out. Just the thought of making money kept me going so I wasn't as committed and every day I had an excuse as to why I couldn't get the work that was set for me done. I have never in my life struggled with anxiety I even feared calling agents.

Napa did mention to me that if I'm doing this for the money then it won't last but if I am doing this because of my WHY?! Then this will always keep me going. Napa did give different approach and constantly shared other people stories to help me overcome fear. But it was actually a mind block. It was not fair on him to waste his time.

I then decided to re-evaluate my why and I figured out that I was chasing the money so when hard work kicked in and there were no rewards yet, I slowed down and disconnected from this strategy.

I can never regret my experience or my journey as I have learnt a lot about myself and met some amazing people along the way. I will definitely be going back to the property world in due time. Once I have strengthened my foundation.

If I started this strategy again, I would create a system that creates more time for my business even if it includes a business partner, does the running around while one arranges the appointments. Spend more time living and enjoying my experience as this build strength. Rather than wanting to keep up with where everyone else is at.

I'll strongly advice you that make sure you are mentally and physically ready as well as the rest. Property is not for the weak hearted you will lose out on time and money. Follow your WHY after you'll get paid for it. Be true to yourself and your business

I spent a lot of time reading about anxiety and this is where I found my purpose on coaching people on mindset. As everything starts from the mind. I have accomplished my first book 'tears of a wounded Mother' that can be found on amazon, and currently writing my second book about how to make your mind work for you. I am a mindset coach and public speaker & have spoken a few panels to empower others to live in their purpose.

Ryan Houten

I am a Scottish guy from a little town called Peebles. I come from a working-class family, being the oldest of 5 children. Money has unsurprisingly, always been tight for us. I hated the worried look I would see on my Mum's face that she might not be able to afford a present for my brother's birthday or that my Dad's annoyed look that we couldn't go to the football match because we were too bloody skint! For as long as I can remember I've had this drive to achieve great things for them.

So, one day when I was doing some "Googling", I saw that most millionaires are made through property. My understanding of property investing was, of course, you needed tens of thousands of pounds to start. Until one day, I discovered the brilliantly clever property strategy known as rent-to-rent requiring little money to start and after I had found that. I wanted someone to teach and mentor me. I came across Napa through seeing him on social media.

My plan at the time was to move to Manchester at some point and start my rent-to-rent business immediately. I messaged Napa and asked him for help. He drove all the way from London to Manchester to come and teach me. We met at one of his rent-to-rent property he just recently picked the keys up for. The training session lasted for a solid 7 hours straight. He covered all aspect on how to start and manage your rent-to-rent business. I was blown away and this guy knows his stuff I thought.

After that day, Napa would be constantly checking up on how my business was getting on. Coaching me how to talk to landlords and agents on the phone. Discussing what problems, I was running into and showing me how to solve them. I knew I could message him whenever I was stuck on something and he'd be right there guiding me through it all.

My original plan of moving to Manchester disappeared and travelling more than 3 hours for viewings was not something I was willing to do. As I was not doing viewings it made it impossible building any relationships with agents or landlords and even making offers. Therefore, that was a major obstacle of me not getting a deal, as I was not viewing enough properties. Since I lived in a village it was not a goldmine that had demand for my clientele.

Everyone at some point will get down and feel all sorry for themselves that they've not achieved their goals in their desired timeframe, when that happens you need go back and reflect on what made you start in the first place. Get hungry again!

Even though I have yet to secure any rent-to-rent deal at the time frame of working with Napa, I am still determined to find proceed on my business once I move to Manchester.

Dominic Adade

Coming from a business background I thought this should be easy right, I was wrong.

My background is in computing, I started my first business which was a cinema in my home country (Ghana). The money generated from my first business I quickly re-invested back to start an internet café that progressed to become a computer school.

I migrated to the UK in March 2014 I was very excited about the move but, saddened to shut down my business for a greater opportunity. To bring financial stability I got a job in security that I did not enjoy, simultaneously, I graved the freedom and flexibility I had in Ghana when I had my own business.

As I was in a foreign land, I started researching different sector of business I could start. I once heard that to be successful you have to model after the successes of others in the field you want to venture.

I stumbled across property investment and attended multiple events and consumed lots of education via YouTube. I decided to join a property academy group ran by a different trainer. I paid £12,000 for the year mentoring however, I did not receive value for money and decided to terminate my agreement with them prematurely.

As I left the academy, I still wanted to work with someone that would be able to guide and support me. I've been following Napa for a while on social media and decided to join his mentoring program. I've received quality training and mentoring from Napa and managed to secure a 6-bedroom HMO property in West London. My emotion got the better of me and took the deal without doing much due diligence. The landlord gave me 15 days grace period to tenant the property and pay full rent after that.

I rapidly jumped online and registered with Spare Room, Open Rent, Gumtree and started a group on Facebook to find tenants, this was great and I found quite a few potential leads who viewed the property, most of them found the bedrooms small, uncomfortable and pricy, others wanted to move in with their partners or children, this would not work for these rooms. Being unable to secure any tenants during the grace period I felt the risk was too high to proceed with this deal and decided to return the keys back to the landlord and walk away. In addition, I lost £1500 during the process.

My biggest obstacle was not finding tenants, taking a property without doing my due diligence of the area and trusting the current operator whom I was taking the deal from. I knew I should do my own detailed due diligence like Napa showed me, but I worked the numbers with what I was told but not what I could get in the area.

Based on this experience I lost interest on doing these types of strategies and planned not to do anything with property until I saved enough to purchase a property.

The capital I invested in this business did not bring me any return and loss me money. As a businessperson I am well aware that not all business will succeed you win some and lose some, however, I am blessed with the knowledge and experience I acquired along the way and the relationships I built.

To anyone looking to go into the property business I will advise to:

1.   Education is the key to unlock the potential this business has to offer so educate yourself well enough

2.   Have a well-structured plan as to what you will do each day

3.   Set achievable goals as to what you want to accomplish in a day, a month, a year, and so on and be prepared to work towards it.

4.   Do your due diligence of the area before you take on a property (obvious right?) if possible, get a property in your area so it's easy to take control of viewings and other challenges that may arise later.

5. Have enough money to pay for at least 2 months' rent to give yourself enough time to find tenants when you find a property

Starting out again if I ever do, I will put in place the above-mentioned points as I have in my new business (funnelworth.com) where we help companies and ordinary individuals build successful and sustainable online business through funnels.

I will also put together offers to ascend my tenants on a value ladder and provide them more value making more money as compared to just putting tenants in the rooms and collecting monthly rents.

I will build an email list of potential tenants and send email follow-ups with images of available rooms for rent since most people are usually uncomfortable in their accommodation and will move if something better comes up.

I hereby close my section with a good luck to any entrepreneur looking to go on this journey and I pray for your success.

Chapter VI

Many are called, few are chosen

*"The external call goes to all people. But only the elect experience the internal call" – **Guy Waters***

I hope reading my mentees experiences on rent-to-rent gave you a feeling and a taste of what is possible. Matthew 5:22,14 says "Many are called but few are chosen". Masses of people are attracted to the rent-to-rent property strategy by the catch phrase NO MONEY DOWN but fail to realise the hard work that is needed when you start this business.

The phrase is also incorrect and quite often resulted in newbies making some serious errors in judgement by failing to secure or save enough money to get started. They are then left disillusioned and upset as they watch their dreams disappear before it began. You will need money to get started in any business. LOW MONEY DOWN is a more apt phrase for the rent-to-rent property business.

For those who decide to be the *chosen ones,* they get to reap the huge rewards rent-to-rent can offer. One common motivation technique that keep my mentees going was knowing their *WHY*; having a purpose and wanting to learn from people who have done it before.

Most people speak in a condescending tone about the rent-to-rent strategy, especially people who are investing in alternative 'low money down' strategies.

People who have embarked on the traditional property investment routes also occasionally try to discredit rent-to-rent as a poor man derivative of the lucrative property industry. The most commonly held belief is that rent-to-rent is just creating another job for yourself.

With rent-to-rent you are effectively becoming a property management company. You are creating a job for yourself by managing the properties you accumulate. The permanence or longevity of the business is solely dependent on your decision to terminate the business or grow it.

To an extent, I may agree with the sentiments expressed above, but rent-to-rent is just like any other business; at the start, the owner has to work hard to build a solid foundation. As the business starts to grow, they can create systems to enable the business to operate successfully with minimal input of their time, effort and money. The business can eventually become self-sustainable.

The majority of people who choose rent-to-rent do not have much cash to invest in asset building strategies.

They may have adverse credit or just want to create a cashflow that would allow them to leave their job.

In the cashflow quadrant created by the author of Rich Dad, Poor Dad Robert-T-Kiyosaki and included below:

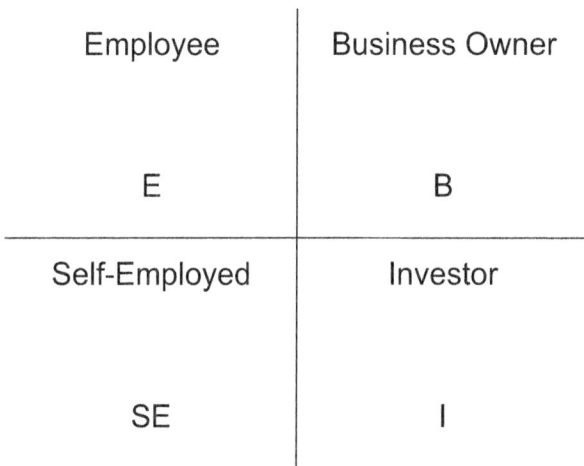

Employee	Business Owner
E	B
Self-Employed	Investor
SE	I

You can work through the cashflow quadrant changing your focus as your business evolve. For example, once you are employed with a company, you can become self-employed part time. Once your part time property business starts making enough money to free you from your employment you can go full time self-employed.

As your business grow you may want to shift to a business owner employing others or act as an investor. I strongly recommend you do not skip the self-employed step as it gives you the knowledge and skills needed to comprehend how your business works and the opportunity to create models that are unique to your business.

When you do have four to five properties you can then start outsourcing jobs to free more of your time and move onto the business section of the quadrant. You can create systems that will work for you and your physical presence is no longer required. When your business starts doing well financially, you can get your money to start working for you by investing in other people's projects. I am now straddling the business owner and investor quadrant. I regularly invest in other business while building my own portfolio.

Contrary to popular belief, other strategies also involve time commitment. If a person chooses the buy-to-let strategy it will require an investment of time to source properties, manage each project and regularly check the property if they live nearby. Like many buy-to-let investors, rent-to-rent investors can opt to outsource the daily management of their properties and free up their time.

When I started my rent-to-rent business, I did everything that was required to make my business a success. I cleaned properties, staged, managed and repaired broken fixtures. It was hard work and extremely time consuming, but it helped me to gain an insight into my business first-hand. Knowledge of the intricacies of my business also enabled me to save money later. I had a five-bedroom HMO and I wanted to employ a cleaner. I invited the cleaner around to visit for a quote and she told me it will take five hours to clean the house. I politely thanked her and showed her the door. I had been cleaning the entire property myself in under two hours.

Do not let anyone tell you that rent-to-rent is just a job because you are only managing properties. In my first book I delved into greater details regarding the entire process of the rent-to-rent journey. In the start-up phase you need to be active learning the ropes and fully grasping your business strategy, unless you have a large budget at your disposal to employ people at the start. After you have established your business you can slowly relinquish control of some aspects of your rent-to-rent business and delegate to employees. Rent-to-rent is not passive at the start, but it has the potential of becoming passive.

Chapter VII

Passive income

*"If you do not find a way to make money while you sleep, you will work until you die." - **Warren Buffet***

Inflation is when money loses value over time and it is happening constantly. There are many economic, social and political factors economist use to determine the rate of inflation but for the average person they measure it using the immediate cost of items or services compared to their net pay. I remember a single bus fare in London was forty pence, now years later the same ride costs one pound and fifty pence.

Interest rates are also calculated using various algorithms and economic factors that is a mystery to many people. What we can all agree on is how low the interest rates on savings are. Most UK bank offer an interest rate of only 0.75%. That is an interest rate in a climate where inflation is 1.5%. You do not need a business qualification to realise that your money in the bank is losing value each year that you keep it locked in a high street bank. Banks are a business and their core objective is to increase profit and grow their customer base. The biggest selling point of a bank is security. Low risk equates to low returns in business circles. To see how banks, use your money, check out the rates they charge on your money when they loan to other people and businesses. What fraction do you receive when your money work in a bank?

Do not be misled into thinking your bank cares for you and your money. They do not. It is just business and you are statistical data. This is your money and it should be working for you and increasing your capital. It should be making you richer, not your bank executives.

On the cashflow quadrant above, the investor is the natural progression from the other three quadrants. Get your money working hard for you rather than you work hard for it.

My company offers opportunities for your money to work for you while you sleep. We offer a higher interest rate on the money you invest with us. We can guarantee to minimally double any interest rate offered by your bank. This is totally passive. No sourcing of properties, no stamp duty, no dealing with estate agents, no project management. You can relax and make extra income on your invested capital. This is another opportunity for you to create another income stream with your capital secured. There is no risk of losing your original investment with us.

The amount of interest earned depends primarily on the amount of money you have invested. A typical monthly return on your investment will be significantly higher investing with us compared with high street banks.

If you are genuinely interested in maximising the interest, you can earn or would like to get more information about our current investment projects and opportunities.

Please use the contact details below to get in touch with me.

Facebook: Napa G Bafikele

Instagram: Napa Bafikele

LinkedIn: Napa Bafikele

Facebook Group: Rent to Rent Blueprint

I would like to thank you for taking your time in reading this book to completion. I really hope it has given you further insights into what it takes to run a rent-to-rent business and how letting your light shine can help those around you.

I want to help as many people as I can to achieve similar outcomes, and if you believe you have what it takes to start your own rent-to-rent business please feel free to contact me.

Make sure you subscribe on my YouTube channel for regular free content.

YouTube: Napa Bafikele.

To find out about my training and mentoring packages please visit www.napabafikele.com

WE COOKIN 🔥 🔥

Sources:

https://hiring.careerbuilder.co.uk/news/almost-one-third-of-british-workers-live-paycheck-to-paycheck-careerbuilder.co.uk-survey-finds

Notes:

Printed in Great Britain
by Amazon